Thirty ...ie New Articles

Articles

An Anglican Landscape of Faith

Martyn Percy

CANTERBURY
PRESS
Norwich

© Martyn Percy 2013

First published in 2013 by the Canterbury Press Norwich
Editorial office
3rd Floor, Invicta House,
108–114 Golden Lane,
London EC1Y 0TG.

Canterbury Press is an imprint of Hymns Ancient & Modern Ltd
(a registered charity)
13A Hellesdon Park Road, Norwich,
Norfolk, NR6 5DR, UK

www.canterburypress.co.uk

British Library Cataloguing in Publication data

A catalogue record for this book is available
from the British Library

978 1 84825 525 8

Typeset by Manila Typesetting Company
Printed and bound in Great Britain by
CPI Group (UK) Ltd, Croydon

Contents

Dedicated to Five Faithful Anglican Sisters:
Ann Verena, Jane Olive, Anne, Mary Stephen, Elizabeth
Jane and to their two Acolytes, Peter and Lister.
May God bless you for your journey of faith and
courage and for settling with us here on the
Holy Hill.

Introduction

Despite the title of this book, this is not about *the* Thirty-Nine
Articles of Religion, as recorded in the *Book of Common Prayer*
(1662). It is, rather, thirty-nine new articles that are centred on
preaching and proclaiming the Christian faith today, and also
offering something of an apologia for the Church. The articles
are primarily (but not exclusively) concerned with the faith of the
Anglican Church. And here I suppose, in that sense, these articles are
not unlike those that still feature in the *Book of Common Prayer* –
articles of or about religion in general, and an attempt to sketch a
specifically Anglican landscape of faith. To be sure, the Anglican
minds that drafted the original Articles sought to articulate a public
and national faith that was broad, generous and inclusive. The fact
that the Church of England was searching out its doctrinal position in relation to the Roman Catholic Church and the continental
Protestants is perhaps significant, in so far as the purpose of the
Articles was to forge some kind of middle ground (or *via media*)
around which a broad range of religious views – which had hith-
erto been competing convictions – could live together in peace. The
Anglican landscape was, from the outset, intended to be a broad
and hospitable environment: there was to be room for all.

Yet the Thirty-Nine Articles have a curious history. The Ten
Articles in 1536, and under Henry VIII's reign, showed notably
Protestant leanings. The revised Six Articles of 1539 swung away
from a Reformed position and back to Catholicism. The Forty-Two
Articles, which emerged during the reign of Edward VI in 1552
and written under the direction of Archbishop Thomas Cranmer,
were intended to summarize Anglican doctrine and saw Calvinist
thought reach a peak. But the death of Edward VI and the reign
of Mary I meant that the Articles were never enforced. It was in

1563 that the Forty-Two Articles became the Thirty-Nine Articles – a Convocation of the Church under the direction of Matthew Parker, Archbishop of Canterbury from 1559 until his death in 1575, failing to pass three of them. Indeed, Anglicans may do well to remember that Church–State relations on matters of religious principle has a long history in England. Elizabeth I reduced the Thirty-Nine Articles by one to thirty-eight – the thirty-ninth only being restored once the Queen's excommunication from Rome had been confirmed. (So forty-two articles are provided here. The final three pieces are more personal in tone, and constitute a set of short supplements, in the way that one might find deleted additional scenes from a film in the subsequent DVD released.)

It is only partially the intention of this book to celebrate the 450th anniversary of the Thirty-Nine Articles of Religion. The original Thirty-Nine Articles were never intended as a complete statement of the Christian faith, but rather to position the Church of England in relation to the Roman Catholic Church and emerging Protestant denominations. The Articles pursued Elizabeth I's agenda, and, in attempting to establish a national church that would maintain the indigenous apostolic faith, incorporated some of the insights drawn from Protestantism, while also being faithful to Catholicism.

The Thirty-Nine Articles enjoy a peculiar status in Anglicanism today. Clergy of the Church of England are required to affirm their loyalty to the Articles; but most Anglican Provinces throughout the Communion make no such requirement. Article VIII states that the three Catholic creeds are a sufficient statement of faith – so it is perhaps strange to then add another thirty-eight affirmations of faith. For many commentators, the Articles are perceived as the nearest thing to a supplementary confession of faith possessed by the tradition. It took some time to draft them (as had been the case with the Six and the Ten Articles), and the process involved dozens of theologians and churchmen over many months. This is perhaps part of the reason why the influence of the Articles on Anglican thought, doctrine and practice remains so profound. The Articles are regularly cited and interpreted in support of doctrine and practice, and sometimes they are used to reaffirm the Anglican comprehensiveness that they strove for in the sixteenth century. One important manifestation of this, for example, is the Chicago-Lambeth Quadrilateral (1886), which incorporated Articles VI, VIII, XXV and XXXVI in a broad articulation of fundamental Anglican identity. But it remains the case that each of the Provinces in the Anglican Communion is free to adopt, adapt and authorize their own official documents. So the Thirty-Nine Articles are not officially normative in all Anglican Churches – but neither is the Athanasian Creed, or the *Book of Common Prayer*.

From the outset, the Articles were intended to blend and balance discipleship, theology and doctrine. This enabled them, at least in theory, to appeal (or to commend themselves) to the broadest domestic audience: Catholic and Protestant. And although Articles are, in some respects, conceptually a rather strange notion for Anglicans today (there being such emphasis on freedom and interpretation in faith), we should perhaps not forget that they were there to provide an open-yet-defined landscape that hosted belief and practice, and not a definitive confessional test for membership. As Thomas McConnell notes:

> The *via media*, in historical terms, was John Donne's phrase whose heritage dates back to Aristotle's 'Golden Mean'. It is striking that in Anglican history, the focus has been on the method, rather than a distinct theology or creed. Perhaps the most important thing about Hooker is that he wrote no *Summa* and composed no *Institutes*, for what he did was to outline method. What is distinctively Anglican then is not a theology but a theological method. (1983, p. 43)

The Articles – tucked away at the back of the *Book of Common Prayer* (1662) – are a revealing window into the ethos of Anglicanism. In particular, they seek to navigate a *via media* between the beliefs and practices of the Roman Catholic Church and of the English Puritans, which in turn gave the Church of England a distinctive character. That is why they deal with anything from preaching and sermons to doctrine and liturgies; and from the status of ministers to the mystery of the Trinity. The evolved and eventual *via media* was expressed so deftly in the Articles that some have labelled their content as an early example of 'Reformed Catholicism'. This is, of course, a compliment to Anglicanism of the highest order. And it perhaps explains why the church – the distinctive form of Anglican Polity – continues to be so influential around the world. It has about 80 million members in 164 countries; so, geographically, it is the most widespread denomination after Roman Catholicism. And although not the largest Protestant denomination, it is arguably, through the legacy of Empire, one of the most influential, largely through its work, schools, welfare and other spheres of mission and ministry. But it is more than the church of the post-colonial British Empire – since more than half of the countries touched by the Anglican Communion were never part of the Commonwealth.

Anglicans, of course, like many global denominations, know a good deal about not getting on too well with each other. The very first Lambeth Conference of the late nineteenth century was rooted in a doctrinal crisis. The twentieth and twenty-first centuries have seen the Anglican Communion at subsequent Lambeth Conferences argue on divorce, contraception, sexuality, gender and other issues. But all denominations squabble – it is a sign of life. Moreover, as Luis Bermejo SJ points out in *The Spirit of Life*, all our creeds were formed through fractious meetings that were rooted in controversy. Christians – and perhaps especially Anglicans – sometimes forget that the Holy Spirit works through meetings (often taking a long time, and over many years); it is how we arrive at truth. Bermejo argues that there are four stages of ecclesial life: communication, conflict, consensus and communion (Bermejo, 1989). Issues in the Anglican Communion tend to get refracted through this fourfold process. This is how the Holy Spirit moves the Church; it is not the case that only the last of these stages – communion – is the 'spiritual' stage. The Holy Spirit is also manifest in pruning and refining in conflict. Thus, Anglicans agree on what the Bible says – but not always on what it means. The polity is often more relational than propositional – Anglicans are often interested in how we disagree, and a little less in what we actually disagree on. As Brian McLaren notes:

> When conceptual agreement fails, [Anglicans] will tell you they are brought together by liturgy . . . but not just words on a page.

Rather, it is their deep appreciation for the deep beauty of liturgy that helps them to make room for one another. (2004, p. 235)

Making room for one another? It doesn't sound like much, on one level. But it is precisely this agenda that forged the Thirty-Nine Articles of Religion. Mclaren is attentive to the fact that Anglicanism is biblical, liturgical, historical, cultural and traditional. It is a denomination rooted in several fusions: Catholic and Protestant; Synodical and Episcopal; open yet defined; concrete and fluid; solid, yet reflexive. The matrix that holds this together makes for a generous ecclesiology and orthodoxy:

> Generous orthodoxy is the practice of dynamic tension: you can resist the reductionist temptation to always choose one thing over another, and you learn to hold two or more things together when necessary . . . Anglicans have demonstrated this both/and beautifully in relation to scripture . . . it is never *sola* [scripture] – never the only factor. Rather, scripture is in dialogue with the tradition, reason and experience . . . None of them *sola* can be the ultimate source of authority . . . When these [the four] agree, Anglicans move forward with confidence . . . When they don't agree, Anglicans seek to live with the tension and the tolerance, believing that better outcomes will follow if they live with the tension rather than resolve it [prematurely?] by rejecting one of the four values . . . all are gifts from God, and none should be rejected . . . Compromise . . . Anglicans make room for one another when scripture, reason, tradition and experience don't line up for everyone the same way. (2004, p. 235)

So what of these thirty-nine articles in this book, 450 years after the original Thirty-Nine Articles of Religion? There are several things to note at the close of this Introduction. First, some of the articles here are very short, and some less so – just like the original Thirty-Nine Articles. For example, Article III (on Christ going down to hell) is a single sentence, compared to Article IX (on original sin) which is a fairly substantial paragraph. Second, the articles here, like the Thirty-Nine Articles, range over religion more generally, but through a particular Anglican lens. This means some articles are specifically about polity, whereas others are about doctrine, faith and Christian discipleship. Third, the articles are drawn from the early years of the twenty-first century, which covers some of the more difficult years in Anglicanism. I simply note that this was not an unfamiliar context for the original Thirty-Nine Articles. Fourth, the articles all share theological and ecclesiological DNA which, although not unique to Anglicanism, is nonetheless found in particular concentrations across the breadth of its polity. That is to say, the relationship between scripture, reason, tradition and culture shapes each article – reflecting one of the core characteristics of Anglican thinking.

Last but not least, a brief word about the origins of the articles in this book, and its overall shape. Approximately half of the articles are drawn from short essays or pieces in the *Guardian*, *Independent* and *Daily Telegraph*, and also BBC Radio Four. The remainder are drawn from homilies at Ripon College, Cuddesdon – a theological college near Oxford preparing women and men for ordained ministry – and are therefore shaped by a formational environment that is focused on a distinctive kind of discipleship. I have felt it right to retain the fairly intimate – and to some extent direct – mode of speech in these sermons and homilies, mindful of how they also speak to others. The original Thirty-Nine Articles of Religion were divided, in compliance with the command of Queen Elizabeth I, into four sections; and I have followed suit. Correspondingly, the structure of the book follows the logic of the listings in 1563: Articles 1–8 were concerned with the Catholic Faith; Articles 9–18 with Personal Religion; Articles 19–31 with Corporate Religion; and Articles 32–39, finally, were deemed to be 'Miscellaneous'. Here, in the final section of this book, I have taken the liberty of celebrating some patron saints and exemplars of the Anglican tradition, some of whom are drawn from the scriptures, and others from history – miscellaneous people. This seemed especially appropriate, given that Anglican faith is learned and lived through practice and example more than in theory. *Lex Orandi, Lex Credendi, Lex Vivendi*: As we Worship, So we Believe, So we Live.

In attempting to follow the outline structure of the original Thirty-Nine Articles in this volume, I have merely sought to honour the genius of the Anglican spirit that brought us such riches 450 years ago and still does so today. Correspondingly, readers may appreciate the listing of the original Thirty-Nine Articles that closes this book. The articles, even today, stand to remind us that Anglican faith remains firmly rooted in scripture, tradition and reason; and was always about Christian practice as much as it was about beliefs. And that just as our faith is formed by the past God gave us, so it continues to shape our present and future.

Martyn Percy
Ripon College, Cuddesdon

Part One: A Catholic Faith

Article One: On Faith in the Holy Trinity

Living the Mystery

With *The Matrix Reloaded* (2003, Fox Studios), Hollywood, that most ardent purveyor of secular discourse, seems to have found religion once again.

Here is a full-frontal exposé of our spiritually saturated, yet opaque, postmodern world, in which we encounter characters called Trinity (a she, by the way) and Neo (a sort of messiah) in their quest for Zion. A computer-generated, virtual reality dark age is battled against by the forces of light, and angels in black leather and shades are pitched against similarly cool demons for the soul of the true world. The film extols the virtues of America's favourite myth: the power of redemptive violence.

For most *Matrix* fans, the religious resonance will be lost. This is a pity, as the scriptwriters have gone to some trouble to offer a tale that could easily be interpreted as a kind of religious pastiche. In particular, it is surprising to see a character named as Trinity. Why? Because few Christians really know what the word means, even though it appears in the creeds and most of our collects.

Yet the word 'Trinity' does not appear in the Bible. Leaving aside the widely discredited reference in 1 John 5.7, there is nothing in scripture that explicitly links together the Father, Son and Holy Ghost. The Christian doctrine of the Trinity was arrived at painfully over 400 years and, like many doctrines, it is a testimony to the partiality of truth as we know and experience it.

It is partly a social consensus bound by time, and partly a political settlement that attempted to bind up arguments and paradoxes to capture the essence of a mystery – something that was glimpsed in a mirror, but only dimly.

The partiality of the witness of scripture is an important key in coming to terms with the Trinity. For the true Christian response to its mystery is not theology or philosophy, but worship. The complexity of the doctrinal formulae points beyond itself. God cannot be seen; his nature is hidden; truth is only dimly perceived.

Thirty years ago, the theologians Daniel Hardy and David Ford suggested that it might be fertile to think of the Trinity as music – most especially as jazz. Their analogy offers an insight into the Trinitarian nature of God: the composer–performer–listener linkage can resonate with the Father, Son and Holy Spirit.

Music is created in time, and yet creates its own time. It involves law and freedom, and its practice reveals more than there is. It is a harmonic language attentive to sadness, celebration, reflection and dynamism. Moreover, music is a gift and, as we learn to understand it, we learn more about the God who has given it.

In thinking about the Trinity analogously as jazz, one becomes mindful of its combinations: its formal dimensions married to its innovative nature, and its capacity to cover a spectrum of needs – from celebration to commiseration. Moreover, there are the many different sounds that make up one sound. Divine music is simultaneously scripted yet improvised; formal, yet free. When the Church corresponds to the Trinity in worship and appreciation, it becomes an orchestra of praise and participation.

Likening the Trinity to jazz is not as strange as it sounds. Jazz is associated with freedom of expression and formality. It is transforming, yet traditional. Order and freedom coexist. From an apparently tense synthesis of composition and improvisation, inspiration, liberation and dance can issue. To worship the Trinity is not to understand each note or to deconstruct the score; it is to listen, learn and participate.

Ultimately, all the doctrine of the Trinity is trying to do is to say something about the abundance of God. All our theology is but intellectual fumbling for truth – a matrix that eludes us. Each insight on the Trinity represents a signpost along the way, yet it is in worshipping the Trinity, not understanding it, that you begin to enter the divine matrix.

Article Two: On Christ, the Son of God

Christ is With Us

Hardly a month goes by without some sort of celebration for a new year. The Church celebrates the turn of the year at Advent, the first Sunday of December. Other religious traditions, with lunar or solar calendars, celebrate their new year at a time that is quite distant from 1 January. Schools and colleges begin their years in September. The financial year of commerce and business often starts on 1 April.

Secular and sacred constructions of time have all found a way of saying 'out with the old and in with the new'. Even in a culture where time is linear and progressive, we need the cyclical rhythm that allows us to break with the past and embrace a new future.

So despite all the partying that surrounds 1 January, it is important to remember that it is an arbitrary date to end one year and to begin another.

Yet the celebration has a pivotal quality. It is a temporal space where people can reflect on what has been, what already is, and what is to come. It is a time to look back, but with an eye on the future. For many, the date marks a time for resolutions; pledges of self-denial and self-improvement briefly abound. People scan astrological predictions, trying to second-guess the coming year. I prefer the Old English proverb: 'Man plans, God laughs.'

For others, 1 January simply marks the end of the annual season for visiting relatives, and ushers in several days of intense consumerism before mundane routines kick in. Sometimes, as in 2004 when the devastating Indian Ocean tsunami killed almost a quarter of a million people, the year ends with tragedy and uncertainty. When lives and futures are swept away by the tides of disaster and tragedy, what is there to hope for as the year turns?

In the Christian calendar, 1 January is also the Feast of the Circumcision, when the Church remembers Mary and Joseph taking Jesus to the temple, in fulfilment of the law. The day reminds us that, in Christian tradition at least, we no longer face the future alone. If the message of Christmas is that God is Emmanuel, 'God with us', then the Feast of the Circumcision is the proof.

Previous generations of Christians attached great importance to the day, for they saw it as the evidence that Jesus really was flesh and blood in a way that his birth had not fully revealed; on this day he bled at the beginning of his life, a sign of his covenant with our lives, and his solidarity with human nature. Here is the first sign that God understands our frailty and pain.

So while welcoming in the New Year, we might reflect on how God has chosen to speak to us. It is a time when many are looking for clear directions or for answers to those questions with which tragedy confronts us. And so it is that in a culture where clarity and certainty are so obviously craved, God reminds us that he has indeed sent us a message.

But it is not one that is easy to read. For it is not a text. Nor is it a clear and obvious clarion call, precisely defining the future. It is, rather, the gift of a child, a baby that giggles, smiles and laughs; and also cries, sucks, pukes, poos and pees.

Is this a joke, I ask myself? That God should come among us not as an articulate adult but in a defenceless, vulnerable form? Yet it is precisely in this unexpected incarnation that the wisdom and love of God is truly revealed.

Here, we come face to face with all that matters. And God laughs, because, as anyone who has ever had a child will tell you, a tiny inarticulate infant is utterly absorbing and demanding. If we can pay attention to that child, the love we give will be returned sevenfold.

But in the meantime, all resolutions and plans are on hold. For God has come among us as a tiny child. And we will have to put time into that relationship if we are ever to hear him speak his first words.

There's a Christmas prayer I love that says 'your cradle was so low that shepherds could yet kneel beside it and look level-eyed into the face of God'. The shepherds did just that. It is what we are invited to do. To look at this child, to ponder this scene, and to see the love of God, for the face of the baby is the face of God. So there are no obvious answers to life's questions at this point. But God does, at least, smile back at us from the cradle.

Article Three: On Going to Hell and Back

The suffering and solidarity of Jesus

'Sticks and stones may break my bones, but words will never hurt me' has never been a true proverb. In a recent survey, swear words and other derogatory terms remain seriously offensive for many people, especially words that slander or malign. The truth is that the words not only hurt; they maim, condemn – and even kill.

One of the more curious features of the Holy Week narratives – normally ignored by the churches – is the amount of swearing and cursing that goes on in the last few chapters of the Gospels. There cannot be much doubt that the Aramaic language of Jesus' time could probably match Anglo-Saxon four-lettered expletives word for word.

Holy Week begins, in Matthew's account, with Jesus cursing a barren fig tree – a cipher for the failure of his audience to realize, and respond to, the good news of the Kingdom of God. Peter, for denying Jesus, 'swears and invokes a curse upon himself'. Jesus stands trial, accused of blasphemy. He, in turn, is insulted and mocked by his Roman guards. Judas knows he is cursed, and hangs himself. And anyway, the problem all began long before this, for 'removing the curse of Adam' is what Good Friday and Easter are supposed to be all about.

The Church has always had a slightly ambivalent attitude towards cursing. The Reformation in England led to the Anglican Church dropping the practice of excommunication, and also disposing of the more ancient services of Malediction or Clamour (meaning 'appeal for justice').

However, the Church of England allowed instead a public reading of Deuteronomy (Chapter 28), within the context of a Service of Commination, which allowed a minister to recite a litany – a general register of God's cursing of certain types of sin and sinners. In medieval and Reformation times, there were also many instances of folk-religion curses – people, in all walks of life, praying for the forces of evil, or the vengeance of God, to be visited upon their enemies and neighbours.

The thinking behind these services, and the more informal practice, was simple enough. If God would bless those whom a blessing was pronounced upon, would he not also curse those who had a curse pronounced upon them?

Modern commentators agree that cursing is an activity that has close associations with blessing. Indeed, the forms of words are frequently parallel. To bless someone, or something, is to raise them, or it, to its proper status before God, enabling fuller praise to be returned through the very thing that is blessed. Cursing is the opposite of this, a spiral of denigration, denial and, finally, the absence of hope.

Like a blessing, a curse is what linguistic scholars term a 'speech act', since it is simultaneously a verbal utterance and a deed performed. In the very act of speaking, there is action. In cursing himself for denying Jesus, Peter attempts to complete his own perception of his separation from God. Likewise, the accusations levelled against Jesus, namely blasphemy, consign him to isolation, and then death.

In all the cursing and swearing of the gospel finales, we are, of course, left with one victim, Jesus, who himself becomes cursed by God – or consigned to evil. But this is not done by words alone; it is the silence from heaven that is deafening and defining. Jesus becomes cursed not by what is said, but by what is left unsaid. And Jesus knows it, too. Abandoned by nearly all to his ignominious fate, he cries, 'My God, my God, why have you forsaken me?'

As Sydney Carter puts it in his hymn, 'The Carpenter', written from the point of view of one of the thieves also executed with Jesus: 'God is up in heaven/and he doesn't do a thing/with a million angels watching/and they never move a wing.' It may seem strange that 'the word made flesh' is finally condemned by God's silence. Yet in a strange way, it is the words of blessing that flow from the dying Jesus that give a clue to what is going on in the crucifixion.

To those who curse and mock Jesus, there are words of forgiveness. For the dying thief, there is an invitation to paradise.

The cross then starts to look like a place of cursing that is turned into something for blessing, and the close link between the two should not surprise us. It is ironic. Jesus, who is the true praise of God, is also, on the cross, the accursed of God. As Carter concludes his hymn, he reminds us of the foolishness of the cross: 'It's God they ought to crucify instead of you and me/I said to the carpenter a-hanging on the tree.'

Precisely. Here hangs one 'who saved others, but cannot save himself'. In choosing to be cursed with betrayal, torture, abandonment and death, the Lamb of God becomes an apparently ordinary scapegoat. Our swearing, cursing and vilification is finally directed against God. And God's response is one of silence and then of blessing.

So, the message of Holy Week is that the cursing directed against one another and against God is wasted, for it is all absorbed in the cross. The cross is itself a speech act – eloquent in its silence, abundant in its proclamation of blessing, and, then again, in its display of love and sacrifice, an utterance and an accomplishment.

The proof of this is in a throwaway remark by Luke, near the end of his Gospel. After the appearance of Jesus on the road to Emmaus, the witnesses scurry back to Jerusalem to proclaim the resurrection. They need not have bothered, for Luke tells us that Jesus has already 'appeared to Peter'.

What words were exchanged between them are not recorded. However, it is safe to assume that Peter, the man who cursed himself for denying any knowledge of Jesus, could begin to understand how this same Jesus, 'the accursed of God', had become the instrument of God's blessing to humanity.

Article Four: On the Resurrection

Bursting our minds

Just before I went to university to read theology, a friend gave me the American author Josh McDowell's book, *Evidence that Demands a Verdict*, which claimed to 'prove' that Jesus had risen from the dead. I was assured that no matter what my lecturers said, this book would help to keep me on the straight and narrow. My friend added that so long as I clung to the truth that Jesus was really alive, I would be able to count myself a 'true' Christian.

More than 30 years on, I can still number myself among the saints. But I have long since abandoned the idea that the Gospels' accounts of the resurrection constitute 'proof' in McDowell's sense. This is not to say that I think that the resurrection stories are analogical or parabolic. They may be; but I also believe they are attempts to proclaim something about real events that burst through every conceivable intellectual and world-view paradigm. Put another way, the words of the Gospels cannot ever do justice to the reality of the resurrection. The first Easter is simply more than tongues can tell.

But there is also a case for saying that the point of Easter is not so much the rolled-away stone, as the carried-away church. Those who want to 'prove' the testimonies as 'facts' have missed something important. The point of Easter is not about attracting punters to peer inside the empty tomb, and persuading them as to the reasons why it is empty. It is about finding and encountering the risen Jesus in the very present.

So, the Easter story is not about proving beyond reasonable doubt that Jesus, who was dead, is now alive. It is, rather, an attempt to show that the 'Jesus project', apparently doomed within the ashes of Good Friday, is somehow born out of the indescribable experiences of the Sunday. To modify a Swedish proverb, good theology is 'poetry plus, not science minus'.

Thank goodness, then, that the Gospels do not end by giving us abstract doctrinal reflections to explain the resurrection. It is a matter of faith, which is why the stories – for all their raggedness, fear, passion and wonder – are the best vehicles Christians have for trying to narrate the first Easter. The advantage of stories is that they give us a kind of deep knowledge that abstract reasoning cannot provide. 'Story knowledge' is also about particularity and exactness – giving us real people doing actual things: going to anoint a body; running from the empty tomb; not recognizing the gardener.

The craving for 'proof', which is bound up with a flawed religious desire to make matters of faith into matters of fact, is as understandable as it is immature. But the need for certainty is not the same as the quest for faith. And Easter reminds us of the power of stories, and the comparative weakness of dogma.

This is because rationality tends to evade the messy particularities of life, pressing on instead to deal directly with the generalized concepts that might lie behind the particulars. As Daniel Taylor (1996) remarks, such an approach often strip-mines reality, washing away tons of seemingly useless details to get to the small golden nuggets of truth. But the truth is in the details, in those vignettes that tell us of wonder, surprise and fear.

The Easter stories, then, are all we have. But they are enough. Never mind that Mark ends by saying that the disciples ran away, or that John records another story that none of the other writers seem to know about. The truth lies in the gaps. The point is that none of these narratives could ever have captured the ultimacy of Jesus on that first Easter Sunday.

But the stories do provide us with clues as to what to expect from the one who was dead, but is now raised. A story of stark absence becomes a story of intense presence. The reality of Jesus is bigger than reality itself. But this is not evidence that demands a verdict. It is a faith, and a new life that invites a response.

New beginnings

Resurrections are disruptive affairs. They confound rather than confirm, leading to that confusing cocktail of emotions, fear and hope.

They sweep away order and reason, leaving the witnesses with no vocabulary and bedraggled by an event that is beyond reality.

As Christians celebrate Easter, the starkness of Lent yields to the sounds of celebration; the cry is 'He is risen', and acclamations of 'Alleluia' ring out from bell towers and congregations of every hue.

But the first Easter was an altogether more confusing and circumspect affair. The Gospels tell us that at the sight of the empty tomb, the disciples fled in fear. And as the appearances of Jesus increased over the following weeks, there were still doubts, questions and more fear. The resurrection broke the world in which the disciples lived, but the new order to which they were beckoned was, as yet, opaque.

In recent years, theologians, bishops and church leaders have found themselves in difficulties affirming what the resurrection is, and what it might mean. For some, the litmus test of orthodoxy has to be a literal affirmation of the historicity of the physical resurrection of Jesus. Anything less is deemed to be dangerous and heterodox. For others, the Gospel accounts can only be the best that language could do to convey an event that was, almost by definition, beyond words.

Yet for all sorts of theological reasons, the resurrection stories are important material to wrestle with. To be sure, the Gospels affirm that Jesus, once dead, is now alive – but he has, at the same time, become an elusive figure. Sometimes present, often absent; sometimes easily recognized, sometimes appearing as a stranger.

Jesus' resurrection provides consolation and mystery in equal measure. In their resurrection accounts, the Gospels seem to be saying something about the very nature of God – that God cannot be pinned down. Recently, a bishop told his diocese that the most perfect image we have of God is Jesus hanging on the cross. Arguably, the plethora of crucifixes in our churches and our culture testifies to the popularity of that sentiment. But can there be a more perfect image of God to behold?

The answer from Easter Sunday to the question posed by Good Friday is an emphatic 'yes'. The most perfect image we have of God is an empty tomb; there is nothing to see, save a few linen cloths on a grave slab. The perfection of this image lies in the very absence of anything to glimpse.

Then there are those two emotions that the resurrection stories evoke: the fear of God (which is the beginning of wisdom), and completely unmerited hope. So the resurrection stories are packed with paradox, not persuasion. It seems that God's style is not to give proof but to pose questions. We are left with clues, not conclusions. The grave clothes are folded neatly, and yet the end of the Gospels are untidy and ragged, as though God could not bear to say 'The End'.

The resurrection stories play with the borders and boundaries of our sense of reality. One minute Jesus cannot be touched (his very instructions to the weeping Mary); the next, he is to be touched (his command to Thomas). And in the middle of this quite human yearn for certainty, Christians are reminded that their religion is, ultimately, a faith, not a science.

So the Easter message is this. The tomb is empty. But there is no point in standing guard outside it, or trying to draw people's attention to the places where Jesus has once been – an empty grave will win few converts. And that is really the point of the Easter story. In the oldest account of the resurrection (by Mark), and in the earliest Greek manuscripts, the Gospel ends mid-sentence, with the innocuous Greek word *gar* (meaning 'for': "they were afraid for . . .").

Thus, a proper conclusion to the story is withheld, and it is up to the reader to say what happens next. The followers of Jesus are invited to write a resurrection conclusion with their own lives.

Article Five: On the Holy Spirit

Pentecost and speaking in tongues

Pentecost commemorates a number of events. Principally, it marks the coming of the Holy Spirit after the resurrection and ascension of Jesus. A frightened group of bereft disciples are suddenly empowered by the Spirit, resulting in the birth of the Church. Luke, the writer of the book of Acts, begins his work by describing the phenomena, the Spirit settling on the disciples like 'tongues of fire'. The disciples become apostles, sealed by the Spirit.

The use of the word 'tongue' is important here, for what follows in the book of Acts provides a narrative link. From tongues of fire, we move to speaking in tongues. According to Luke, the disciples are able to stand before a vast and cosmopolitan crowd, and address each person in their own language. Suddenly, the apostles become multi-lingual, with the gospel being preached in Latin, Greek and the like.

Like me, you may have questions about the story, as well as the general phenomenon of speaking in tongues. And you are not alone. Although Pentecostalism and Revivalism claim to practise the art, the origin, use and interpretation of speaking in tongues requires more careful explication.

A preliminary observation to note here is that the account in the book of Acts can be read analogically. In the Old Testament (Genesis 11), the story of the Tower at Shinar tells of how all the different languages in the world came to be. Once upon a time, all nations spoke with one voice. But then people got ideas above their station, and decided to build a tower to heaven, in order to get on God's level. God, who liked his privacy and primacy, sowed dissension among the ranks of builders by inventing new languages that hampered the construction. Shinar became Babel, from which we derive the English word 'babble'. Not for the last time, an ambitious building project is scuppered through poor communication.

The account in Acts is probably an attempt to redeem and reconfigure this fable. The message is this. In the Church – a construction of the Spirit – all languages are recognized and spoken. The Spirit is universal, not local: the gospel is for all people. So, the first act of the Spirit is to reverse the tragedy of Babel: God now speaks to everyone, and the Church becomes a global *lingua*. The language is that of the Spirit.

It is important not to take the account in Acts too literally. When early Pentecostal missionaries thought they had received the gift of tongues at the turn of the twentieth century, they often assumed they were beginning to speak a new language that would enable them to preach the gospel in some far-flung corner of the globe. At the end of the century, more sober scholarship and reflection has drawn back from this.

On the matter of complete languages being spoken by people who have never learned them, most Pentecostal scholars now agree that there is no hard evidence of anyone miraculously receiving Arabic, French or Spanish directly from the Spirit, as the book of Acts implies.

Academics in the field of consciousness studies also point out that you could not confidently speak a language you had never learned. Otherwise, how would you know you were saying 'Jesus is Lord' instead of 'Haddock and chips, please?'

I don't mean to mock. The more common tradition of speaking in tongues is that which Paul describes as 'sighs and sounds too deep for words'. But most linguists and psychologists agree that whatever these 'tongues' are, they do not add up to a language. It is more like an ecstatic utterance, a kind of 'sound salad' that is full of feeling and meaning, but with no vocabulary, grammar or anything else that could enable it to be translated. It is the articulation of the unutterable.

A teacher of mine who specialized in primal religion, and spoke the languages of the people he studied, would sometimes spend his sabbaticals visiting charismatic churches. When the time came to prophesy, he would often chip in, and speak one of the primal languages he knew so well. Congregations were invariably impressed and, without fail, his words were usually interpreted by someone 'led by the Spirit' – as a prophecy for the church, or a word of encouragement. But in actual fact, he was simply repeating a recipe for a type of corn porridge, made out of goat stock. This seems a bit cruel now, in retrospect. But the point he was making was a sincere one: tongues, whatever they are, are not languages in the way that we conventionally understand them. Tongues are, rather, sighs and groans too deep for words. They are modes of communication that defy translation.

But in interpreting tongues for our own time, what are we to say about deep and mystical experiences that seem to defy description – let alone clarification or understanding? I speak from personal experience, as one who found myself experiencing an intense spiritual epiphany at the shrine of St Frideswyde.

Granted, I can make some sense of that experience. I was baptized at one of the very few churches dedicated to her shortly before my first birthday. The graphic spiritual experience seemed to centre on the relationship between the water of baptism and the healing water she once drew from a well. But I cannot, I'm afraid, communicate in words anything of the intense, compelling and deep nature of what I felt on that afternoon that reduced me to my knees and rooted me to the spot. It just happened: it was undeniable.

So, what might tongues and Pentecost mean for us? I'd like to make a couple of brief observations to help us in our reflections. First, and as I have already implied, I do not consider the gift of tongues to be a 'language', but rather a kind of 'overflow' of praise; a release of the heart and mind when words will no longer do. As the French sociologist Danielle Hervieu-Leger puts it:

One could ask whether the search for . . . non-verbal forms of emotive communication does not also express a protest against the stereotype nature of approved religious language, something about the diminished quality of articulate religious quality in modern culture. The place taken in these groups by the gift of tongues raises the questions directly . . . tongues, defined by scholars as 'phonologically structured human expression without meaning, which the speaker takes to be a real language but which in fact bears no resemblance to any language, living or dead', is not a vehicle for communication but for *expression*. The content is of little importance: tongues find [their] meaning

not in what is said but in the very fact of speaking and respond-
ing, in this form, to an immediate experience of great emotional
intensity. In the emotive response there is a general sensation of
the presence of the divine, profound joy, and inward well-being
which finds the means of expressing itself. (2000, p.59)

As one modern poet, Kei Miller, puts it:

> years later a friend tells me
> tongues is nothing but gibberish – the deluded
> pulling words out of the dust. I want to ask him
> what is language but a sound we christen?
> I would invite him to a tent where women
> are tearing their stockings, are on the ground
> pulling up fresh words to offer as doves to Jehovah.
> I would ask him if he sees no meaning here
> and if he never had the urge to grunt
> an entirely new sound . . .

(Miller, 'Speaking in Tongues', 2007)

Second, the gift of tongues reminds us that God – who was and is
incarnate in Christ – remains radically available in our contexts
and language: we hear the gospel in a tongue we can understand.
This is important, for we can appreciate how easy it is to exclude
all kinds of 'minority interests' in the Church. Black, lesbian, gay,
feminist and other kinds of theology or Christian expression, for
example, can be narrated as substandard or even offensive 'dia-
lects', marginalizing them as 'bad language' over and against the
suspect claim that the Church has one true language. Moreover
(and perhaps tellingly for the Anglican Communion), the biblical
text suggests that although the apostles spoke to their international
audience 'each in their own tongue', it doesn't follow that the
apostles necessarily understood one another at the same time. In
fact, the message of Pentecost is that there are many tongues of fire.
And because much is lost in translation, the hermeneutical task of
the Church – what one theologian memorably describes as 'reach-

ing across distances' – becomes even more urgent. The Caribbean theologian Kortright Davis expresses it simply enough:

> Western theologians are [now] attempting to educate themselves about the new theological surges emanating from the Third World. They have finally realized that there is no universal theology; that theological norms arise out of the context in which one is called to live out one's faith; that theology is therefore not culture free; that the foundations on which theological structures are built are actually not transferable from one context to another. Thus, although the gospel remains the same from place to place, the means by which the gospel is understood and articulated will differ considerably through circumstances no less valid and no less authentic. (1990, p. 70)

Quite so. Put another way, we might say that the lesson from Pentecost is that theology (or Christianity) is always spoken in tongues, so that each can understand in their own language (but, by the way, not necessarily one another). There is no Christianity that lacks a local accent; there is no one, singular 'pure' version. Theology and faith is always contextual, but that does not suggest an ultimate capitulation to eventual relativism.

On the contrary, the Pentecost experience can set the soul alight, so that the tongues produced themselves become mystical vehicles that produce harmony, unity and creativity. But we have to work on translation and interpretation in the meantime. In short, tongues of fire, flickering in the Babel of modernity (making sounds of significance in a world where mere words are losing their power), point us forward. These are the signs and groans that are too deep for words. This is God's jazz: composition and improvisation blended together in dynamic spiritual overflow and praise. Text, music and tradition combine as the Spirit blows where it wills. We wait for the birth of an age to come: where all shall eventually see, speak and understand – face to face, each in their own tongue.

Article Six: On the Scriptures

How does God speak?

Teabing smiled. 'Everything you need to know about the Bible can be summed up by the great Canon Dr Martyn Percy.' Teabing cleared his throat and declared, 'The Bible did not arrive by fax from heaven . . . the Bible is a product of *man*, my dear. Not of God. The Bible did not fall magically from the clouds. Man created it as a historical record of tumultuous times, and it has evolved through countless translations and revisions. History has never had a definitive version of the book . . . More than eighty gospels were considered for the New Testament, and yet only [four] were chosen for inclusion . . . The Bible, as we know it today, was collated by the pagan Roman emperor Constantine the Great.' (Brown, 2003, pp. 230–1)

Speaking as the person quoted above, I guess I ought to clarify my views a little more. It is true that 'the Bible is not a fax from heaven' is a quote correctly attributed to me, although, to the best of my knowledge, I have only ever said this in lectures, radio, TV and newspaper interviews – all in connection with understanding fundamentalism. But behind the slick sound bite, there is in fact a fairly sophisticated theological point. Let me explain.

Views about the authority and status of scripture cannot be directly resourced from the Bible itself. The Bible has no self-conscious identity. As a collation of books and writings, it did indeed come together over a long period of time. Indeed, the word 'Bible' comes from the Greek *biblos*, simply meaning 'books'. Equally, the word 'canon' (here used in relation to scripture, not as an ecclesiastical title) simply means rule. So the Bible is, literally, 'authorized books'. But as I say, the authorization of the compilation took place after the books were written. It should be clear that Paul, when he wrote 'all scripture is inspired by God' (2 Timothy 3.16) in a letter to his friend, Timothy, could hardly have had his own letter in mind at the time. The conferral of canonical status on his letter came later – some would say much later.

My point is simple. Views about the authority and status of the Bible cannot be solely resourced from the Bible. The Bible needs to be held and understood in a particular way, independent of its content, in order to have any authority. Furthermore, behind such a view is some kind of nascent notion of how the power of God works in the world. For some (perhaps especially fundamentalists), the power of God must be mediated through clear, pure and easily identifiable channels or agents. This guarantees the quality of that power: it is unquestionable and unambiguous. As one exponent of the 'fax theory' puts it:

> God caused to be written precisely what He wised, and His words were in no way altered or corrupted by the human agent through whom they were written down; so that we have no right to say of anything in Scripture that it is merely a human idea and not part of God's word. (Packer, 1958)

But for others – usually of a more mainstream, broad or perhaps liberal persuasion – God acts and speaks through channels and agents that are fully themselves. So God works through culture, peoples and history, not over and against them. Correspondingly, the power of God is only ever known provisionally (not absolutely); it can only be encountered 'through a glass darkly', and not 'face to face'. Thus, although the power of God may be pure and absolute at source, God *always* chooses to mediate that power through less than perfect agents (such as language, people, times and places). And this is because God's primary interest is in disclosing his love in order to draw us into relationships, and not in unequivocal demonstrations of power, which would leave no room for a genuinely free response, but merely obedience in the face of oppression. So we have the burning bush for Moses – but he covers his face. And although Jesus is the light of the world, 'the darkness comprehendeth it not', according to John. What is revealed is still 'hidden' to those who are blind.

But how does the 'fax' quote relate to the Bible? Simple. Some Christians believe that scripture has come from heaven to earth, in an unimpaired, totally unambiguous form. Such views are fundamentalistic: the Bible is the pure word of God – every letter and syllable is 'God breathed'. So there is no room for questions; knowledge replaces faith. It is utterly authoritative: to question the Bible is tantamount to questioning God.

But to those who believe that scripture is a more complex nexus of writings, the authority of scripture lies in the totality of its inspiration. Thus, the Bible does indeed contain many things that God may want to say to humanity (and they are to be heeded and followed). But it also contains opinions about God (even one or two moans and complaints – see the Psalms); it contains allegory, parables, humour, histories and debates. The nature of the Bible invites us to contemplate the very many ways in which God speaks to us. The Bible is not one message spoken by one voice. It is, rather, symphonic in character – a restless and inspiring chorus of testaments, whose authority rests upon its very plurality.

So, when Paul tells us in 2 Timothy 3.16 that 'all scripture is inspired by God', he is not talking about himself. For the early Christians, the 'scripture' Paul refers to may have meant the Old Testament, and perhaps what they knew of the Gospels. But it didn't mean the New Testament, because as a settled volume or concept, it did not exist until the fourth century, the same time the creeds crystallized. But is it true to say that the New Testament is 'the work of man'? In one sense, yes: people had to write the texts – they were not faxed! But on the other hand, there is a case for arguing that the Church only chose authentic and faithful records that testified to Jesus accurately, and history bears this out. As Michael Ramsay remarked, 'The Bible is a consequence of Christianity, not its cause.'

And that is why, in places, including the Gospels (*pace*, 'the synoptic problem'), scripture is sometimes a conflictual dialogue. We are drawn into a mystery and conversation with God, not given a fax of plain instructions. In a similar vein, David Brown notes:

in the Bible and beyond more often than not truth has emerged through lively *disagreement*, and not simply by formal acceptance of an existing deposit or simple deductions from it. The ability to envisage alternative scenarios has thus always been integral to the healthy development of the tradition. Unilinear theories of development must therefore be abandoned, and the search for consensus *within* conflict be taken with much more serious-ness, whether we are thinking of later church history or even the Bible itself. (2000, p. 26)

But what does any of this have to do with us today? The answer, I guess, is in what we make of this curious word we use all the time about quite a lot of things – a kind of fluid currency, if you will. The word is, of course, 'inspiration', which in its original Greek usage literally meant 'god-breathed' – *theopneustos*.

There are many kinds of inspiration, naturally; but the question arises, what kinds of inspiration does God use? A burning bush may seem 'obvious' to you: but to others? Remember Elizabeth Barrett Browning's poem:

Earth's crammed with heaven,
And every common bush afire with God;
But only he who sees, takes off his shoes –
The rest sit round it and pluck blackberries. (Browning, 2008)

The verses are in their own way inspired; but they are also about inspiration. They play with light and dark, with what is hidden and revealed. Like a good inspired text, the poem doesn't *tell* us what is happening, but rather draws us in together, asking: 'What do you see?' 'What does this mean?' 'What do I understand?' They help to make, in other words, *a community of interpretation and apprecia-tion*, gathered around signs, symbols and words or art. In George Herbert's memorable poem, interestingly using the word 'scriptures' rather than the singular, he writes about the complexity, breadth and richness of the Bible. It is so much, and does so much:

Oh Book! infinite sweetnesse! let my heart
  Suck ev'ry letter, and a hony gain,
  Precious for any grief in any part;
To cleare the breast, to mollifie all pain.

Thou art all health, health thriving till it make
   A full eternitie: thou art a masse
   Of strange delights, where we may wish & take.
Ladies, look here; this is the thankfull glasse,

That mends the lookers eyes: this is the well
   That washes what it shows. Who can indeare
   Thy praise too much? thou art heav'ns Lidger here,
Working against the states of death and hell.

   Thou art joyes handsell: heav'n lies flat in thee,
   Subject to ev'ry mounters bended knee.

II

Oh that I knew how all thy lights combine,
   And the configurations of their glorie!
   Seeing not only how each verse doth shine,
But all the constellations of the storie.

This verse marks that, and both do make a motion
   Unto a third, that ten leaves off doth lie:
   Then as dispersed herbs do watch a potion,
These three make up some Christians destinie:

Such are thy secrets, which my life makes good,
   And comments on thee: for in ev'ry thing
   Thy words do finde me out, & parallels bring,
And in another make me understood.

   Starres are poore books, & oftentimes do misse:
   This book of starres lights to eternall blisse.

(Herbert, 'The Holy Scriptures', from *The Temple*, 1633)

Inspiration, then, is not about restating the obvious. It is about receiving the breath of God; hearing his whisper; seeing his shadow. So scripture – like art, music, poetry, symbols and signs – invites us to sit awhile and contemplate. The burning bush of Moses has no single meaning. It is an invitation to pause and look more closely; step through the gates of mystery that God provides for each of us. It is in contemplation that we find depth and wisdom; and with that, love and breadth. God did not send us a fax, but rather his son, born of a woman. The Bible, we are reminded, is a unique star:

> Starres are poore books, & oftentimes do misse:
> This book of starres lights to eternall blisse.

The light shines and the fire burns; and some people are struck by its beams of radiance. But the rest, as Browning says, carry on picking blackberries.

Article Seven: On Vocations

Offering up ourselves

Readings: Isaiah 6.1–8 and Mark 1.14–20

A vocation is not a career, but a life surrendered to God. Every Christian has a vocation. But just as every life is unique, so is every calling. No two are identical, and while you can often discern clear patterns and several similarities, in the end it comes down to each individual, their relationship with God, and then to the wider Church and world. Wisdom, the mystics tell us, is knowing your place before God. And a vocation is about finding that place, and then knowing what to do next.

But it is never clear cut. As Woody Allen once quipped, if you want to make God laugh, just tell him about your future plans. Vocations can be quirky, unsettling and uncertain. For most people it's not a question of hearing a clear voice from heaven, but rather piecing together shards of evidence: insights, affirmations and nudges from all over. It can take years to discern.

And callings aren't always instantly recognizable. It is pretty typical of God, if you think about it. He comes to us in unexpected ways: a child in a manger, a still small voice, a thick silence, a bush alight. Not all signs are easy to read. And this is perhaps what Isaiah is wrestling with when he sees his vision of God (Isaiah 6.1–8). It ends with the oft repeated rhetorical question: 'Whom shall I send; who will go for us? Here am I. Send me.'

'Send me'? Surely God is kidding. There must be better qualified, nicer folk that God could choose, reasons Isaiah. But the invitation is clear. It resonates with some words Jesus will utter to his disciples hundreds of years later: 'You did not choose me; I chose you.' Which is why a vocation is not like a career. It is simply a life surrendered to God.

Like Isaiah, we often cannot fathom God's wisdom, or his reasoning. But vocations often start in marginal places and with ephemeral events. God, the seemingly capricious conductor, seems to orchestrate vocations in unusual ways. As one poet, Emily Dickinson, puts it, truth is often a superb surprise – because 'the truth must dazzle gradually, or every man be blind'. Vocations often sneak up on us. Others see them in us before we do. Few are granted the blinding light. A vocation is simply what happens when we stop running, and surrender ourselves to God.

One of the really arresting things about Mark's Gospel is that you never get time to settle. You don't have the luxury of the well-drawn-out and skillfully crafted stories of Matthew and Luke, or the long conversations and dialogues that John gives us. With Mark, you are straight into the action, and then onto the next scene. And then the next. It is breathless.

The good news is here, now. And it requires your immediate attention, and a response. Here, now. So the tone of abruptness in the message of Mark is also his theme. There is no time to cogitate and deliberate. Choose Jesus. Drop everything you are doing, right now, and follow him. Come.

Yet what is so intriguing about Jesus is the range of people he chose to share in this work. It included women and men – and not all of great repute – along with fishermen, tax-collectors and others. The ensemble was hardly the cutting edge of leadership and eloquence. Yet in choosing widely, we gain a foretaste of what the Kingdom will be like, and the Church might become: a place both of diversity and unity; a true home for all.

And this is why vocations are so diverse. God does not call any one 'type'. God calls all types. Some are gifted in particular ways; others bring different talents to the table. But as Ephesians 4 suggests, the gifts are not competitive, but rather complementary. The gifts are bestowed from grace, so all may be of benefit. The unity of the Church flows from diversity, not uniformity. So from the very beginning of the Gospels, the story about vocations is a testimony to the extraordinary range of people that God uses to share in the work of the Kingdom.

Vocations often come gradually – emerging from the dawns and dusks of our experiences. It was a gradual illumination that eventually made some sense to me. I had no thoughts of ministry or priesthood until I was in my mid-teens. I first twigged that I might be called to ministry when I was 16 – a rebellious, recalcitrant and slightly reckless youth. Perhaps not quite the teenager from hell, but definitely one that knew how to put his parents through some purgatory. Despairing of their eldest son, my parents made me sit a two-day multiple-choice career test to help determine my future. The theory was that if I had a goal in life, I might actually take aim at something.

And what did the random-tick-this-box-careers-test conclude might lie ahead? First, consider a career in teaching. (This pleased me – a chance to get my own back on the system.) And the second option was to consider becoming a clergyman. This idea horrified me, truly. But I could not shake it off. Try as I might to leave it, it would not leave me.

It was to be another ten years before I was ordained. And that time and space was important. Vocations are rarely sudden, complete epiphanies. It takes time to come to a mind, for the heart to be still, and for the soul to be attuned. But as far as God is concerned with vocations, you can run all you like, but you can't hide. Vocations can be like the proverbial Hound of Heaven from Francis Thompson's wonderful poem:

I fled Him, down the nights and down the days;
I fled Him, down the arches of the years;
I fled Him, down the labyrinthine ways . . .
From those strong Feet that followed, followed after . . .
(Thompson, 1998)

But if it is true that every Christian has a vocation, what are the next steps? How would you know you were called? How could you be sure? You can't of course, but there are a few simple things to bear in mind.

First, have courage. Many vocations never take root because of fear. Fear of failure, or perhaps just of getting it wrong – suppose someone rumbles that I am just ordinary? Suppose I really make a mess of it? But mistakes happen, and I think the best thing we can try to do is learn from these things. Failure is not the worst thing; letting it defeat you is. It takes a special kind of wisdom and courage to face failure and defeat, and then to try and move on from this.

Second, have patience. The Christian life is a marathon, not a sprint. And vocations are weighed and measured over the entire course of a life, not just a few moments of success or glory. It takes a long time to appreciate just how much God has called us to. It takes daily devotion to see that our calling is not about affirmation or success, but rather faithfulness. We are not primarily called to win things – even for God – but simply to *walk* with Christ.

Third, have humility. A vocation is not about the trappings of power and privilege in ministry. The gospel is always about eternal rewards, not the temporal baubles of the Church. The call is that we have our eyes fixed on Jesus, who is, by the way, coming back to do an audit. We do not, therefore, need our focus to be on a career path. Ultimately, a true vocation is something of a release – not something that is to be grasped.

This why the apostle Paul's well-known phrase is so vital to remember: 'his power is made perfect in our weakness'. We do not belong to a faith where power finds expression in perfectionism. Or where our vocations – whatever they may be – raise us up several feet beyond contradiction. Rather, we look for the God who is incarnate, who comes to the world, and is found in human form. God *uses* our weaknesses – the foolish and base things of the world – to bring about change. Which is why he says to each and every one of us today, as he did to the fisherman at the beginning of Mark's Gospel: 'Come, follow me.'

Article Eight: On Believing in the Church

Anglican life and catholic identity

An apocryphal tale tells of someone writing to the Archbishop of Canterbury to thank him for something he had said on the radio. The correspondent kindly enclosed a cheque for £10, made payable to 'the Church of England'. But it could not be cashed, for there is no organization or bank account bearing that name. True, there is the Church of England Pensions Board, various divisions concerned with ministry and education, several dozen dioceses, and of course the Church Commissioners – all of which refer to the Church of England. But no bank account bears the sole nomenclature. The cheque had to be returned with a note: 'Thank you – but could you be more specific?'

It is perhaps no accident that when Jesus turned his mind to the subject of the Church, he used a rather riveting analogy: 'I am the vine, you are the branches.' Even for an apparently homogeneous organization like the Church of England (let alone the Anglican Communion), 'branches' offers a better descriptive fit than most of the labels on offer. It suggests intra-dependence yet difference; unity and diversity; commonality yet independence; continuity and change; pruning yet fruitfulness.

In other words, the analogy sets up a correlation between particularity and catholicity. This is, of course, a struggle that Anglicans are all too familiar with. There is a constant wrestling for the 'true' identity of Anglicanism. The Church finds itself easy prey to a variety of interest-led groups (from the theological left and right) that continually assert their freedoms over any uneasy consensus. The assumption made here is that any one branch is 'free' from the others.

Technically, this is correct. But the illusion of independence threatens to impoverish a profound catholic aspect of Anglicanism. The right to express and practise particularity is too often preferred to the self-restraint hinted at by a deeper catholicity. Thus, one branch will exercise its assumed privilege of freedom – fiscal, political, theological or moral – over the others. The consequence is that the branches attempt to define the vine.

This is why issues of gender, sexuality and polity quickly become the primary focuses that distinguish one branch from another, rather than secondary indicators of emphasis subjugated to an innate connectedness to the true vine. There seems little understanding that an unfettered claim to act freely can become antisocial, or even unethical. Great freedom comes with great responsibility.

Bishops have a vital role here in presiding over diversity while maintaining unity. This is why the key to some of the current divisive Anglican dilemmas may lie in dioceses and provinces becoming more expressive of their catholic identity, and celebrating their coherence amid their diversity. A diocese is part of a larger, organic whole – a branch of the vine. Therefore, exercising its freedom and expressing its particularity is less important than maintaining its connectedness. Naturally, such restraint need not impose limits on diversity. It merely asks that the consequences of exercising one's freedom be more fully weighed.

Whenever Anglican leaders meet, there is much to contemplate: how to hold together amid tense, even bitter, diversity; how to be one, yet many; how to be faithfully catholic, yet authentically local. In all of this, an ethic of shared restraint – born out of a deep catholicity – may have much to offer the Anglican Communion. Without this, Anglicans risk being painfully lost in the issues that beset the Church, unable to see the wood for the trees. Or perhaps, as Jesus might have said, unable to see the vine for the branches.

Part Two: Personal Religion

Article Nine: On Sin

All desires known?

There is a clothing shop in Oxford market that sells T-shirts with some quite excellent religious messages. Particular favourites include 'I have found Jesus!' with, in small letters underneath, 'He was down the back of the sofa all the time'. Or, 'God loves everyone' with, in small print, 'but I'm his favourite!' And appropriately for the season of Advent, there is 'Jesus is coming! Quick, look busy.'

Advent is that time in the Christian calendar that marks the start of the Christian year by anticipating the end of history. This is the moment in time when time will be no more; when, lo, he will come with clouds descending, with angels and trumpets in accompaniment, to wrap up the history of earth and fold it into the eternal history of heaven. Traditionally, therefore, Christians have used Advent to prepare. The four weeks before Christmas are punctuated with acts of penitence, abstinence and self-examination. But just when the whole world seems to be caught up in the feverish consumerism of Christmas preparations, the Church has a hard task in trying to persuade us that this is a time to pause, and to think about the judgement that is to come.

Setting aside most of December as a period of penitence and holy preparation seems almost risibly counter-cultural. Most of us don't like churches that bang on about sin too much. In our therapeutically attuned culture, the very concept has been somewhat downgraded. Sin may induce guilt and shame. Such concepts, we are frequently assured, are paralysing and unhealthy.

A recent local survey of children's attitudes to sin suggested that the concept is becoming rather outmoded. Even the children from quite religious families struggled to explain what sin was. One child said biting his sister was 'bad', another that jumping on the sofa was 'naughty'. And from their schools the children seemed to have learned that the great evils of the day are global warming, pollution and bullying. And the answers to these vices? Take more care of the world, be nice to other people and be sure to recycle.

A culture formed mainly out of desire and achievement may find itself in the grip of a subtle temptation, namely to confuse sin with imperfection, with what we lack as people. To be sure, it is often helpful to be conscious of sins of omission and negligence. Yet a society that plays down the idea of serious personal and social sin, and even apparently unfashionable concepts such as original sin, does so at its peril. For in ignoring the dark side of human nature we risk collapsing into a falsely optimistic world-view that then struggles to cope with the reality of evil when it strikes. Rather than accepting sin as commonplace, we have presumed to regard the state as exceptional, and even as a private matter.

I suspect that part of the problem lies in language. Sin is a short, simple word – perhaps too easy and quick to utter. The very accessibility of the word has arguably played a part in the weakening of its power. Our older and arguably denser religious vocabulary preferred the word 'trespass'. The word captures the idea that lines have been crossed, that some of the things we say, do and think are actually offensive, and grieve God.

Cranmer's majestic Collect for Purity in the *Book of Common Prayer* understood that a great deal of sin is concealed inside us:

> Almighty God, unto whom all hearts are open, and all desires known, cleanse the thoughts of our hearts by the inspiration of thy Holy Spirit . . .

All desires known? And in the run-up to Christmas? Seriously? Does God really know what I want, and what I desire? Yes. To God all hearts are indeed open, replete with their miscible emotions and motives. And all our desires are known too, with no secrets hidden. All of them are seen by the one who is returning. Yet the prayer continues, in petition, 'cleanse the thoughts of our hearts by the inspiration of thy Holy Spirit'.

A prayer for the cleansing of desire seems an appropriate way to approach the clutter and gluttonous onslaught of the Christmas consumer-fest. But it also captures something of the Advent hope: that light can pierce the darkness, purity trounce pollution, salvation overcome sin. Advent, then, is a serious time of preparation. For Christmas, yes. But also for the rest of our lives, and beyond.

Article Ten: On Fathering

Joseph and Jesus

In our household we don't do very much about Father's Day. My sons seem to think that on the day in question, I should be bestowing gifts on them. I recently got a homemade card. 'No point in buying one;' said my wife, 'that just feeds the commercialism of a wholly contrived celebration that is only designed to line the pockets of card manufacturers.'

'I couldn't agree more,' I sighed.

Unlike Mothering Sunday, there is no Fathering Sunday in the Church. Mothering Sunday is one of those festivals that conveys myriad meanings. The mothering of God and the Church as mother are linked to values and virtues such as nurture, tenderness and empathy. But what can be said for Father's Day? Is there anything within the Christian tradition that might give a cultural celebration a bit of a spiritual boost? Possibly.

Step forward Joseph, the husband of Mary, Jesus' (step-) father and an odd choice for a Christian model of fathering. Yet there is potential here. Joseph accepted Jesus as his son. He is a model of adoption, embodying the triumph of grace, where nurture is placed before nature; father to a child that is not his kin.

Yet the Gospels are reticent about Joseph. He seems to vanish after Jesus' childhood. But his initial impact on the Christian story should not be overlooked. Joseph puts child and mother before his reputation, making a family where there could have been a simple absence.

According to Margaret Visser in *The Geometry of Love*, medieval portrayals of Joseph tended to denigrate rather than celebrate the man, but Joseph's reputation began to rise in the sixteenth century. He became patron saint of a few countries, and of the Church itself in 1870.

But it is as St Joseph the Worker that he has come to be best known, and in many countries this association is celebrated on May Day. Joseph emerges as the solid type: faithful, dependable, providing as father and husband. It is perhaps for this reason that Joseph is the patron saint of priests – those fathers, at least in the Roman Catholic tradition, who are also non-fathers.

In other words, there is a lot more to fathering than any biological act. Fathering can mean transcending familial boundaries, fostering values that are shared out beyond biological families. This life and graciousness can help model different types of community, and point towards a more open society.

I speak from experience. As an adopted child, I am aware of the love and acceptance given by a father and mother who are not my biological parents. Nurture triumphs over nature once more; generosity over genes.

Yet I am also aware of the lengths my 'birth father' went to ensure that my 'birth mother' was well cared for. Their relationship fizzled out before I was born, and yet both acted with integrity in the adoption process. Perhaps they saw – granted, earlier than most have to face this – that parenting might sometimes mean letting go rather than holding fast.

This is a lesson that Luke's Gospel says Mary and Joseph learned when Jesus was about 12. Like many children on the verge of adulthood, Jesus starts to develop a mind of his own, and becomes prone to wandering off. For Jesus, the elders and scribes of the temple were more intriguing company than his parents. He simply dismisses Mary and Joseph with 'Did you not know that I must be about my father's business?' So we have another slight for Joseph, which he no doubt took on the chin, as any petulant prodigy's father must learn to bear.

More poignantly, perhaps, the theologian Gareth Jones's poem ('Games and Stories', 2013) imagines Joseph, the adoptive father of Jesus, constantly caring for his son over many years. Indeed, the genius of Jones's poem is that he imagines Joseph living throughout the ministry of Jesus, and so present at the crucifixion, resurrection and ascension. Joseph is therefore caught up in the web of deep care, love and anxiety that every parent knows only too well, and at times consumes any father with what almost seems like possessiveness:

I could not bear the horror of my love.
I lost you in the crowds:
Small, slow, already gone.
I lost you in the hills, Sea, towns.
Not really lost; found.

I lost you in the Desert. Forty days
And nights, searching:
Until I found you, brought you
Home: my son.

Once I lost you in the Temple, my
Tiny, marvellous boy, full of
Games and stories.

Yesterday I lost you to the air.
Raised up. Knowing:
I cannot bear the horror of my love.

Which returns me to my Father's Day which, rather like Mothering Sunday, can point towards all those relationships that construe society, and then invite deeper reflection upon the values that we associate with fathering. How my sons remember me as a father will matter. What my sons might pass on to their own children, and to society more generally, is what Father's Day should be all about. I hope and pray that their memories will be as rich as my own were. And I thank God for Joseph's fatherly care for Jesus.

Article Eleven: On Mothering

The mother of all days

It is important to distinguish Mothering Sunday – which marks the mid-point in Lent – from its more recent incarnation as Mother's Day (or Mom's Day in North America, Australia and New Zealand), which is largely a mishmash of sentiment, and with some debt to commerce.

It was probably the Victorians, spurred on by the greeting card industry, in an unholy alliance with florists and confectioners, who divorced the sacred from the secular. In the past, however, the day was used to visit your cathedral, or 'mother church', tying the pilgrimage in with the set gospel reading for the day, which recalls that 'Jerusalem is the mother of us all' (Galatians 4.26).

Traditionally, that visit was accompanied by relaxations of the penitential observances of Lent. This gave rise to the day also being known as Refreshment Sunday, which was marked by putting aside the sombre purple or unbleached linen clerical vestments, and the wearing of rose pink garments instead. Some Anglo-Catholic churches continue to observe this tradition.

Yet there are deeper sociological and theological reasons why Mothering Sunday connects us to other truths that are sometimes lost in today's world. Three, in particular, come to mind.

First, mothering does not always come from nature, as any fostered or adopted child can testify. Mothering Sunday is thus a reminder of the priority of nurture over nature.

Second, there is a strong theological tradition that emphasizes Jesus and God as being mother-like, an aspect of our imagination that has been repressed by the establishment of God as 'male' and 'father'. Yet for medieval mystics, like Bernard of Clairvaux, feeding off Christ's blood was like suckling God's breast milk; it nourished the soul. As Anselm (AD 1033–1109, and an Archbishop of Canterbury) says in his devotional writing: 'But you Jesus, good Lord, are you not also our mother? Are you not the mother who, like a hen, collects her chickens under her wings?'

Third, a concentration on God or Jesus as mother had profound implications for the structuring of ecclesial authority in medieval Christendom. Indeed, focusing on the origin of Mothering Sunday can help to overturn the patriarchy that has been so inimical within Christian institutions. True, the centrality of Mary has celebrated the various virtues of motherhood, but it has still tended to ascribe a subordinate, even passive, role to women.

Yet those who once led monastic communities, including men like Bernard of Clairvaux, were keen to promote their leadership in terms of being 'mothers' of their communities, not just fathers. For Bernard and his contemporaries, the maternal imagery offered a way of ordering relationships within monastic communities.

Correspondingly, terms like 'mother', 'nurse', 'breast', 'womb' and 'feed' were words that carried a particular authority for religious leaders that transcended gender, for they were linked to education, formation and the very life of faith. Thus, to a novice he fears has departed the monastery for the world, Bernard of Clairvaux writes: 'I nourished you with milk while yet a child – it was all you could take. But alas, how soon and how early you were weaned. Sadly, I weep, not for my lost labour but for the unhappy state of my lost child – torn from my breast, cut from my womb (Letters 1.10).'

So Mothering Sunday is about celebrating the deeper virtues of motherhood, and the ways in which God's care and love for humanity are profoundly mother-like. If celebrated truly, it restores motherhood to a real place of authority in the Church, home and society. After all, where would any of us be without mothers? And how would any of us develop without being well mothered?

Article Twelve: On Children

The life of God's family

Can you spot the connection between Moses, Muhammad and Jesus? They are all great religious leaders, all champion a monotheistic tradition, and all hail from the Middle East. But there is a deeper tie that binds them together: they are all, in some sense, adopted.

Moses was abandoned by his birth mother in a coracle on the Nile, and had the good fortune to be picked up and nurtured by a pharaoh's daughter. Muhammad was orphaned as a child, and brought up by his uncle. Nor was Jesus, according to Christian orthodoxy, exactly the child of Joseph.

When most people think about adoption, they believe it is the child who has been rescued, and that adoptive parents are the redeemers. Yet, in three of the world's great religions, this equation is turned around so that the adopted child becomes the redeemer, or the gift.

This is particularly true in Christian thinking, where orthodoxy teaches a kind of double adoption. One human family takes Jesus to themselves in less than ideal circumstances; in return for God's adoption of us by Jesus, we are ourselves adopted into the life of God.

The plight of Mary and Joseph, and the birth of Jesus, still has a resonance in many societies. An unwanted pregnancy can be problematic at the best of times. Bringing up a child that is not your own is not a modern problem. Yet in close-knit communities, and in previous generations, a child born outside marriage could bring disgrace.

It is to this potential disgrace that adoption brings something new: giftedness. Any adoptive parent will tell you that the real winner in the process is not the child, but the one who has gained the child, and what that person brings to that family or to that couple over the years.

In spite of many childless couples seeking babies to adopt, adoption is becoming less popular than it once was. Many older children live in care for years for want of a home; many modern families avoid the risks, opportunities and disruptions that adoption or fostering can bring. In spite of families becoming more diverse, definitions of 'nuclear' or 'ideal' or 'normal' families have become more constrained, even narrower.

It is sobering then, to remember that God's redemption, as portrayed in the Bible, often comes through unconventional families, and through breaking old family patterns. God seldom uses 'nice and normal' families to accomplish his purposes. Time and again, he uses the unconventional, the marginalized and the ostracized to bring fresh revelation, breaking down old social and moral codes.

Today, as in the Bible, families who welcome strangers into their midst, and who share their lives with those who are not their own, say something profound about the priority of humanity, community and personhood. The act of adoption marks us out as individuals and communities for whom nurture is ultimately more important than nature, whereby love and generosity transcend genetic identity.

In Christian orthodoxy, it is commonplace to speak about the incarnation as some kind of risk. God's risk in becoming human – thereby risking rejection and alienation. Moses and Muhammad underwent different kinds of adoption, but each was also with risk. Yet in each case, the risk was taken not just because someone thought there was a divine plan, but because the risk was enacted among a community of gracious human beings – an uncle, the pharaoh's daughter or a peasant Palestinian girl and her distraught fiancé. This is not just about parenting: it is about receptivity to the other, and a willingness to share your life.

Of course, this begs all kinds of questions about the limits we place on the identity of a typical family. Some of these are appropriate, to be sure. But there are also some that might confine and stifle some of the other creative and fluid models of family life we see expressed in scripture. I believe that adoption is an active verb rather than a noun – that is to say, that each of us needs to look at how we adopt those around us who may have needs, or may be dependent, whether they are related to us or not.

Adoption is not an isolated event that individuals once undertook. It is a process of life in which all can participate, and in which the desire to nurture is crowned by the willingness ultimately to set people free, no matter how costly that may be. Most adopters and adoptees would agree; they would say that they are all the richer for it.

Article Thirteen: On Ministry

Preparing pastors

Reading: Luke 16.1–13

> Man of theology, man of reconciliation, man of prayer, man of the Eucharist; displaying, enabling, involving the life of the Church – such is the ordained priest. I have not made 'pastor' one of the categories, because pastor describes the whole. (Ramsey, 1972)

What does it mean to enter into training and formation for ministry? However you look at it, this period is transitional. It is neither the beginning nor the end; the destination or the starting place. To begin training and formation for ministry is to embrace gestation. Environments that seek to prepare women and men for ministry are like wombs – places of nourishment and growth – that will, in time, give birth to the vocation. It is no accident that the word 'seminary' is linked to seeding and insemination. Seminaries are, literally, breeding grounds.

But ask anyone in a seminary, 'What's it like?', and you are bound to get some odd answers. Some might say it is a Vicar Factory. Others, that it is an ivory tower, unrelated to the real world. Others, that it is a kind of Holy Hogwarts: a place of preparation for ecclesiastical wizardry. But so far as God is concerned, such places – however they are named or nicknamed – are places of preparation, growth and nourishment.

These are the places where God can feed and challenge us in encounters and engagements that will help to shape and form us into the people he wants us to be. And I don't say this from any particularly privileged position. We are all God's 'work in progress' here. We are not complete, and we don't seek to be the perfecting agents working on the imperfect. We are in this together, and we look forward to learning with you on your journey. This is partly why we remember that ministry and priesthood is 'much more than a set of competencies. No accumulation of skills impresses God. God is interested in the heart of the priest, more than how impressive his or her CV appears to be' (Pritchard, 2006, p. 4).

That's right. But we do well to remember too that the theological study is not a distraction for our hearts – it is food for them. This is why study is so important for one's formation. And it takes awhile to align the study and the worship, the journey and the thinking, the practical and the theoretical. They all belong together, even if at first it seems like you can't see the wood for the trees. Trust me when I say that working through this will be worth it. It will bring wisdom and perspective, and depth . . . and joy.

But to embark on the journey, you'll need some stamina too. One of my favourite American writers, Anne Lamott, tells of how she says the Daily Office each and every day – but a shortened version. Morning Prayer consists of a one-word prayer: 'whatever'. And Evening Prayer a two-word intercession: 'Ah, well . . .'. Well, we all have days like that, especially when the workload seems overwhelming and the tasks fruitless. But she also has some other advice for us:

> Thirty years ago my older brother, who was ten years old at the time, was trying to get a report written that he'd had three months to write. It was due in the next day. We were out at the family cabin in Bolinas, and he was at the kitchen table, close to tears, surrounded by binder, paper and pencils and unopened books on birds, immobilised by the hugeness of the task ahead. Then my father sat down beside him, put his arm around my brother's shoulder, and said, 'Bird by bird, buddy. Just take it bird by bird.' (Lamott, 1995, p. 33)

Perspective, then, is needed. We all need support. The time ahead is one where shrewdness and management – to borrow two concepts from our Gospel today – are needed. Harness your energies to do what is required – and God will do the rest.

So, where do you fit in with all of this now? What is going to happen during this period of training and formation? Allow me to suggest that one of the dynamics that takes place during our time here is that we learn to find ourselves in God's orchestra. One writer puts it like this:

Christian leaders are like conductors of God's local orchestra. Our task is multi-layered. We have to interpret the music of the gospel to bring out all its richness and textures and glorious melodies. We have ourselves to be students of the music, always learning, and sharing, with the orchestra what both we and they have learned about this beautiful music. We have to help members of the orchestra to hear each other, and to be aware of each other as they play their 'instrument' or use their gift. Without that sensitivity to each other both an orchestra and a church descend into a cacophony of conflicting noises. (Pritchard, 2006, pp.109ff.)

I'd like to continue with this analogy, and make some key observations. First, whatever part you play in the orchestra, try and pay attention to the bass line, and don't get overly distracted by the melody. The bass line is all about patience, depth and pace. It is about developing sustainable rhythm for the entire symphony – not just the short movement in which you might mainly feature. Second, just as scripture is symphonic in character – many different sounds making a single, complex, but beautiful melody – so is God's Church. And our task is to try and help you play beautifully, perform faithfully . . . and within the context of the diversity of the many different sounds and notes that God gives us to make, together, something much richer. So listen to one another. Pay attention to the cadence, timbre and rhythm of what we are about. And listen for that greater sound . . . and the signs and notes of the Spirit, too deep for words.

The story of the calculating steward in Luke 16 reminds us to be pragmatic, and to try and balance our commitments. It also suggests that God will use our shrewdness, our resources, and even our weaknesses, to get things done. There is a great deal to do, and much lies ahead. But if you take anything away from this gospel story, remember that God is always looking for our faithfulness. If you serve God with your heart, mind and body, your vocation will grow and flourish.

So, let the music begin. And may the God who has equipped you already, give us all the love, strength and wisdom we need for the journey ahead. He who called us shall surely be with us. He is faithful. Now and always.

Article Fourteen: On Patience, Hope and Love

Learning, loving and leaving

Readings: Romans 8.18–25 and I Corinthians 13.

One of my favourite children's books is *Jasper's Beanstalk* by Neil Butterworth and Mick Inkpen. Jasper plants the bean and has various problems with trying to make it grow. He encounters slugs, snails and worms. It shows the different stages of growing a bean and gives valuable lessons in life processes and cycles. But the primary message of the book can be summed up in one simple word: patience. For our hero, Jasper – a cat, by the way – plants his beans, and simply cannot wait for the results. He plants Monday. He waters Tuesday. But when nothing happens by Wednesday, he digs up the bean and has another crack, and then another, and then another, before finally giving up, and simply tossing the useless bean away. Whereupon, of course, it falls into the ground, germinates and eventually gets its chance to grow into a giant beanstalk.

The lesson for ministry, and in developing a vocation, could hardly be more instructive. What is planted today does not necessarily sprout tomorrow. The harvest may indeed take its sweet time to come. And it is no good being impatient. Just wait, and see.

Our scriptures have much to say about patience. Yet we assume all too often that it is a passive kind of waiting; a form of restraint in which we simply bide our time before we get the result we either wanted or didn't want. But patience is no such thing. It is being still before God, and realizing that in the waiting, all desires are known, transformed and reshaped. In the activity of patience – a virtue and a discipline – we discover that God does things with us in the space. Things gestate, germinate and grow; we find that we acquire a new wisdom. In the waiting, and in Godly patience, we discover new things that would not be seen had we just hurried by.

It may seem strange, but God can do some pretty good things with apparently unpromising material. Some of the things, like Jasper's bean, are full of all the right potential. But what they need is time and space to grow, and a little bit of patient husbandry. What is needed is the wisdom to wait, attentively, for the signs. Of course, one cannot simply wait for ever. But in any case, we don't. For the scriptures assure us that 'we wait in hope' – for what we cannot yet see, but what will be (Romans 8.25).

So let me say a bit more about patience, hope and love. For I truly believe that more than anything else, this is what our Anglican Communion yearns for at the moment; and it is also what our churches need from their ministers. There is a palpable longing for hope and change these days. Jim Wallis comments:

> Hope is the very dynamic of history. Hope is the engine of change. Hope is the energy of transformation. Things that seem possible, reasonable, understandable, even logical in hindsight ... often seemed quite impossible, unreasonable, nonsensical, and illogical when we were looking ahead to them. The changes, the possibilities, the opportunities, the surprises that no one or very few would even have imagined become history after they've occurred.
>
> Between impossibility and possibility, there is a door, the door of hope. And the possibility of history's transformation lies through that door .... Spiritual visionaries have often been the first to walk through that door, because in order to walk through it, first you have to see it, and then you have to believe that something lies on the other side. (Wallis, 1994, pp. 238–40)

There is plenty of hoping and waiting in the practice of Christian ministry. They are about a furtherance of that work that God began in us before we even knew it. Bishop Peter Selby suggests that this gestation – a pregnancy if you will – is all about the future hope:

> what love does do is make space for the unknowable possibilities which the future holds for those who know the history

of love as revealed in the dealings God has had with God's people – patient, kind, ready to excuse, to trust, to hope, and to endure whatever comes ... We are to be towards one another as those who do not know or own each other's future, except that it is in the hands of the One who has proved trustworthy in the past. (Selby, 1997, pp. 64–65)

Love, then, does not end. It is attentive and watchful, hoping and waiting. It is proactive patience, not just passive. In waiting for God's time – *kairos* – we set aside our sense of time – *chronos* – so that God can meet us how we are, and change the what, why and where we are. Sometimes this can be frustrating – for we long for change. But God, in his wisdom, longs to reconcile all things, and so is prepared to wait – sometimes a very long time. And as the mystics say, God has only one weakness: his heart – it is too soft.

Knowing this, and practising God's time, requires a fusion of wisdom, virtue and discipline. It is often expressed and practised formationally in the phrase *feste lente* – make haste slowly. Sometimes the pause is more pregnant and profound than the action. Here is what Rowan Williams, reflecting on being in New York close to the Twin Towers as they collapsed, has to say about Jesus apparently doing nothing, when everyone wanted him to act, speak and judge there and then. But he does not. He pauses, writing in the dust:

What on earth is he doing? Commentators have had plenty of suggestions, but there is one meaning that seems obvious to me in light of what I think we learned that morning. He hesitates. He does not draw the line, fix an interpretation, tell the woman who she is and what her fate should be. He allows a moment, a longish moment, in which people are given time to see themselves differently. (Williams, 2002, pp. 78–80)

It seems to me that the two great besetting sins of the Church these days are impatience and procrastination. The Church either moves too quickly, and then regrets the unforeseen consequences. Or it moves so slowly or not at all, with all the activity and energy of a hibernating tortoise. And many in ministry – indeed, perhaps all of us – oscillate between action and inaction, impatience and procrastination. So you'd think that the art of ministry is all about striking the right note of compromise. But it really isn't.

Good ministry is, in the end, not finding the middle ground between action and inaction, or decision and indecision. It is about knowing your place before God, and being a person of character and virtue – 'marked' and 'formed', as it were, by Christ's life, and living out his goodness. It is about hope, love, grace, understanding, counsel, strength, depth, lightness, prayer, wisdom and humanity in the midst of it all. It is not about compromising between extremes; it is about living authentically in the midst of the place where God has set you.

So what is my hope for the Church, and for those God has called to ministry, as they go forward? It is that we will all have the wisdom, patience, hope and love that is needed for the long road ahead. And that we will be able to wait for God's good time, and also be able to see where he is working before, in and ahead of us. It is humbling, to be sure. But be assured, hope is all about the things we do not yet see.

Ultimately, a church without patience is a church without hope. And that is why, when Paul talks about patience, hope and charity – a wonderful trinity of virtues – we often focus on love, but underestimate patience and hope at our peril. Patience and hope may be the best of these things after all: it is at least close run – and, of course, not a competition. So, as we move forward, and prepare to become servants and leaders of the Church, remember this.

Vocations begin with patience. And God will bless vocations in their time of gestation. Correspondingly, we are to be patient with the people whom God has called us to serve. We of course hope that they will be patient with us. We need to learn and re-learn to be patient with God, and God, in his wisdom, will be patient with us. Because God is love: he believes and hopes all things for us and for his Church. It is always worth the wait. Patience is always rewarded. Because we always wait in hope, and because God is good. And if you can be hopeful, patient and good – trust me – all shall be well.

Article Fifteen: On Interruption

Beginning with God

According to the theologian Johannes Baptist Metz, there is a single-word definition for religion: 'interruption'. I suppose it could equally be disruption – but it isn't. To interrupt means to pause, set aside. Ponder. Stop. And that, I suppose, is what we are asked to do when we enter a period of training and formation. Pause. Look around you. And make the most of the time and the space. It will be busy, to be sure. But if you let it bud and flower, you will also find it a place of peace. You are being interrupted.

Indeed, such a time might even become a profound moment of stillness – a rare and precious gift. A life and a vocation with no space and no still point will need some hard pruning if it is to grow into its proper shape. 'Nothing in all creation', says Meister Eckhart, 'is so like God in stillness.' It is in the stillness that we find something more, something deeper, and a new clarity as we worship a mystery. 'Mystery', mind, when applied to God and the things of God, does not mean a cryptic puzzle that we might one day be clever enough to solve – especially if we do well in theology! Rather, mystery indicates that there are truths beyond the limit of our finite and feeble minds. Some things will only be understood in silence, love, contemplation, compassion, mercy and worship. It is surprising, I think, how few of the things that are learnt in a theological college can actually be taught.

Wisdom is often attained through the learning we gain from suffering, struggle and even bereavement. We become wise not only by what we might know – but also by becoming more tolerant, compassionate, hopeful and humble. Moreover, it is through thankfulness and gratitude – Eucharist literally means 'thanksgiving' – that we discover more of the abundance of God, his grace and his infinite wisdom. That is why the point of training is not to succeed;

but rather, to worship and wonder at the surprising and surpassing God who called you to ministry and, for awhile, to a place apart.

So, during this time, be kind to yourself. Compassion, just like charity, begins at home. Have mercy on yourself. You will not master everything. And it is a kind of blasphemy to view ourselves with so little compassion or such severity, when God already looks on us with such love. This is often our stumbling block – especially in places that can sometimes seem critical and competitive. But in a phrase of Tillich, we have to learn to accept that we are accepted. We begin with grace.

So the faith we seek to cultivate is not really about finessing or finishing. Nor is it about assenting to new theological formulae. There is plenty to be learnt, to be sure – and time for that. But at the core of a community of formation there is a deep commitment to helping you with, and holding you in, your relationship with God – and this is reciprocal and shared. Like every living relationship, it has to be worked on; and the experience of a lifetime will refine, challenge, change and deepen what we have.

Prayer, then, is not an escape from life – a few minutes to plea bargain with God, and then return to reality. Prayer is, rather, a disciplined and regular reminder that we always live in the presence of God. And because we can marvel that his love in Christ is constant and total, we find that thankfulness is the only true response to that reality and mystery, which holds us in our very being.

That is why good prayer is, fundamentally, a constant state of gratitude. Thank you for this day. Thank you for rest and sleep. Thank you for this food. Thank you for this place. Thank you for what has been. And for what is to come. As Eckhart says, if the only prayer you ever say in your life is 'thank you', it will be enough. This is the essence of the meditation from Ecclesiastes (1.2–11) on wisdom and life, and of the Gospel, which asks the teasing question put on the lips of Herod, 'Who is this Jesus that we hear so much about?' This is what formation helps us find out. Wisdom, life and who Jesus is will do just fine.

Which brings us, neatly enough, to two things we all struggle with: theology and the Church. Theology first. Theology is, I suppose, primarily speaking and writing about God. But since God is by definition not available for inspection as an object in the laboratory, this entails speaking about the imprint of God on human lives – and thus about what humanity looks like when exposed to an active, intelligent, transcendent reality. Formation is all about discerning the imprint, and dwelling with the mystery. It requires time, attention and patience – and it will have its frustrations, as much as its epiphanies and joys. But let it be – it will take its time to work in you.

This is perhaps an unusual way of describing theology. Yes, there is content. But some of what we learn has to be apprehended and comprehended on spiritual and intuitive levels; it can be instinctive and a matter of the heart, as much as the head. This is why we tend to talk about formation, rather than simply filling with knowledge; why exploration, a sense of wonder, and a cultivation of the soul can be as important as anything we might do with our minds in the brain gym. As one poet, Brian Patten, puts it:

When I was a child I sat an exam.
This test was so simple
There was no way I could fail.
Q1. Describe the taste of the Moon.
It tastes like Creation I wrote,
it has the flavour of starlight.
Q2. What colour is Love?
Love is the colour of the water a man
lost in the desert finds, I wrote.
Q3. Why do snowflakes melt?
I wrote, they melt because they fall
on to the warm tongue of God.
There were other questions.
They were as simple.
I described the grief of Adam
when he was expelled from Eden.
I wrote down the exact weight of
an elephant's dream.
Yet today, many years later,
For my living I sweep the streets
or clean out the toilets of the fat
hotels.

Why? Because constantly I failed
my exams.
Why? Well, let me set a test.
Q1. How large is a child's
imagination?
Q2. How shallow is the soul of the
Minister for Exams?

(Brian Patten, 'Minister for Exams', 1996)

Then, second, there is worship. Let me get the key question on the table from the outset: why does Jesus want us to do something that is often quite tedious? Some people love ritual and are never so happy as when they put on odd clothes and process round churches. I am not one of these. I understand the disquiet of those who find ritual impersonal, frigid and often boring. I identified with the man who was woken by his mother one Sunday. 'Get up, it is time to go to Mass.' No reaction. Ten minutes later she was back again: 'Get out of bed and be off to church.' 'Oh Mother, why should I?' 'For two reasons. You know that you are supposed to go to church on a Sunday. And, secondly, you are the bishop of the diocese!'

As Timothy Radcliffe OP says, the church has a concrete wisdom. Its central act of worship, the Eucharist, is a discrete and subtle drama. It has three acts, focusing on faith, hope and love. The first act forms us as people of faith. We declare our belief in God's unconditional love and mercy; we open our ears to hear God's Word, and then we confess our faith in the Creed. The second act takes us through the desolation of the Last Supper, when nothing seemed to lie ahead except Golgotha. There seemed no future. In this dark moment Jesus performed a gesture of hope, sharing the bread and saying, 'This is my body given for you.' Faith overflows into hope. And the final act draws us together into communion, which is the victory of life over death and of love over hatred. Hope flowers into Easter love. And it is in that love that we are sent out at the end of the Eucharist to be bearers of the good news.

To be sure, the Eucharist is not always experienced as dramatic. We are not always filled with ecstatic joy. Indeed we may have the impression that nothing much happens. But like formation – our yielding to a process that comes through vocation – the really profound transformations of who we are occur in the depths of our being, gradually and imperceptibly transforming our humanity. May it be so for us all.

Article Sixteen: On Transformation

Walking with God

Reading: Mark 9.30–37.

Committing ourselves to a new future in which there are risks and uncertainties is something few of us relish. Yet it is a daily reality for us all. It is often necessary to make a distinction between real and illusory religion. It is tempting at such times to cling to comforting certainties and false hopes. Yet we know that deep down, the future is open, and that sating the craving for certainty is no substitute for faith. The philosopher John Macmurray tells us that the maxim of illusory religion runs like this: 'Fear not; trust in God and he will see that none of these things you fear will happen to you.' But that of real religion is quite contrary: 'Fear not; the things you are afraid of are quite likely to happen to you – but they are nothing to be afraid of.'

Perhaps our best-known psalm, the twenty-third, captures the essence of our assurance. God will be with us – in whatever shadows or valleys we walk through. But we are never offered a detour. There is no way around the difficulties we face in life. Rather, Christian faith offers a way through these things. So as we face the challenges and opportunities of new starts, we step out in trust and in hope. We don't know what our future looks like. But we don't need to, either. As one poet and philosopher put it, many years ago:

> I said to the man
> who stood at the gate of the year,
> 'Give me a light that I may tread safely
> into the unknown.'
> And he replied,
> 'Go out into the darkness

and put your hand into the hand of God.
That shall be to you
better than light
and safer than a known way.'
So I went forth
and finding the hand of God,
trod gladly into the night .
(Minnie Louise Haskins, 1875–1957)

One of the great conundrums that faces all those who find themselves caught up in or called into ecclesial life is how to resolve
questions of authority and power. And the great temptation –
always, I think – is to try and resolve the miscibility of ecclesial
life with a clarity that ends up oppressing more than it frees, of
being bondage more than liberty.

In Mark 9.30–37, the disciples, arguing over their respective status on the road to Capernaum are, I think, well motivated. They are
doubtless looking at the motley crew that Jesus has assembled, and
have quickly concluded that what is needed is structure, leadership,
clear lines of authority and appropriate concentrations of power in
persons and offices. And as they are the first to have this epiphany,
they naturally nominate themselves. It does not seem to be such a
bad idea. It is tempting, too, just to look around you for a moment.
You can understand why God called you to be where you are – and
my, hasn't he equipped you well? But as for one or two of your
neighbours, well, I am sure God can see the potential. But maybe
you can't quite . . .

Moreover, such 'problems' in ecclesial life have continued to
germinate well beyond the New Testament. Christians agree about
what the Bible says, but not what it means. And the resolution
to this dilemma, at least apparently for some, is to have leaders
who can proscribe the meaning. After all, why settle for confusion
when you can apparently have clarity? Yet Jesus' response to this
is to refuse and rebuke the choice between clarity and confusion.
Instead, he draws us quite properly to complexity.

Which is why Jesus deals with the argument the disciples are
having in two complementary ways. First, by pointing out that the
leader will suffer and die. And second, by picking up a child, and

setting the infant in the midst of the group, and reminding everyone that the leader will be the one whose attention is fixed upon the most innocent and vulnerable in our society, and not on those who merely aspire to high office. So, by drawing their and our attention to the topsy-turvy world of the Church, Jesus changes the way we look at each other, and at God. Leaders must be servants. Teachers must be learners. Rulers must be slaves. It is complex; and not as simple as it seems.

In other words, Jesus will not adopt the hierarchy 'of the gentiles'. The Kingdom he preaches and practises will be riddled with teasing contractions, and knotty dilemmas. It will be the proverbial Gordian knot; but not one that you can cut through.

I often admire the patience and composure of church leaders, who when pressed to be assertive and directive on delicate or controversial matters find the grace and strength to hold back. Some call this weakness, dithering or foolishness. But it seldom is. For such leaders, in practising hesitancy (or willed spiritual patience), allow the necessary space to develop which permits discussion and deliberation – even if it might call into question their own power, authority and leadership.

Secure in what they are called to, they do not need to 'lord it over' anyone; nor do they need to assert their primacy. They let the space become. And the Church then breathes, even as it finds its voice – and might begin to argue.

But this is, of course, not a bad thing. Christians, like all human beings, disagree. That is in the nature of collective and social gatherings. The moral question for Christians is not 'Why do we not agree?' (it is inevitable we sometimes won't), but, rather, 'How do we disagree?' How do we conduct ourselves? With assertive power and oppressive authority? Or with dignity, patience and humility?

Jesus speaks tenderly and graciously to the disciples. He does not chide them for their ambition; nor, indeed for their nascent vocation to leadership. Rather, he gently reframes their desires. The Kingdom of God will be led by acts of service, humility and the practice of virtues. Jesus says that the leadership he is looking for will often *not* be clear, directive, structured and concrete. We simply won't be able to get the kind of clarity that the disciples suppose is needed.

Rather, the life of the Kingdom and the Church is bound to be one of messy contingency; a miscible muddle in which things will get done by love, service, grace and gentleness. Sometimes there will be decisions, and leaps forward; and leaders may take us there. But most of the Church is about love and service; the practice of virtues and the raising up of exemplary lives of holiness, charity, hope, faith and deep spiritual joy. This is what James has to say in our Epistle: 'this wisdom from above is pure, then peaceable, gentle, willing to yield, full of mercy and good fruits, without a trace of partiality or hypocrisy.'

And when you perceive this, you won't want a place on the left or the right of Jesus, staring down at your adoring flock of submissive and compliant devotees. You'll want to be on your knees, towel in hand, with a bowl of water at your side.

Article Seventeen: On Identity

The Jesus question

Strange though this may sound, the two key questions that face each and every one at theological college are these: Who do you say that I am? And, by the way, who the heck am I? It would be rather odd seminarians that did not find themselves asking these questions at some, or several, points during their training and formation. For the essence of training and formation is to undergo something of a transition – to move from cherished spiritual securities and favoured faith foundations into new, strange and unfamiliar theological territory. It can be disarming, and unsettling. Old routines that got you here – for so long the manna that sustained you on the journey – are suddenly disrupted by new patterns of worship, prayer and study.

Understandably, many object to this. Theological colleges can quickly become places that are characterized – unfairly as it happens – as venues that foster doubt, nourish vagueness, and even corrode faith. Yet I want to suggest that this journey – one of movement from security to the uncertainty that accompanies exploration – is precisely where God wants us to be. For he teaches us often and best when we are at our most open.

The Australian theologian and educationalist Denham Grierson (1985) says that this process of 'de-tribalization' is 'alarming to some, threatening to most and determining for all'. He likens it to joining an army: stripped of our former identity, with new codes, rules and uniforms, we are re-educated and disciplined in a new kind of personal and collective responsibility. Grierson makes a good point, albeit and arguably too strongly. We are about to become estranged from our immediate past; and this is part of what God has called us to at this time. We are going to be formed and re-formed.

But let me offer some comfort also. Seminary is a *transitional* phase. This is a time for change and renewal. And although the repercussions should be evident for many years to come, and welcome at that, some sort of balance is restored. You will be able to say who you are. And also who Jesus is. This is a time, therefore, of intense journeying. And it is worth going with the flow. There will be thrills, and disorientation. But let the journey come to you. And try and find some peace and space in this time of training to reflect on who you are, what God has called you to, what you are becoming, and who Jesus was, is and is becoming to you.

Lancelot Andrewes, Bishop of Winchester, was one of the great Caroline Divines of his age, and a profound spiritual writer. His prayers and sermons were hugely influential and inspiring in their day, and for many continue to be so. Andrewes knew something about the unpredictability of the Christian journey, and he has some advice for us that captures something of how we might prepare for a time of training and formation. He too knows that when we find we are losing ourselves (to God), we have nothing to fear, and much to gain:

> Thou art careful about many things: but one thing is needful.
> We will give ourselves continually to prayer and to the ministry of the word.
> Love the Lord all thy life and call upon him for thy salvation.
> A man (or woman) can receive nothing except it be given.
> More is done by groanings than by words: to this end Christ groaned, to give us an ensample of groaning.
> It is not that God desireth us to be suppliant or loveth that we lie prostrate: the profit thereof is ours and it hath regard to our advantage.
> Prayer goeth up, pity cometh down.
> God's grace is richer than prayer:
> God always giveth more than he is asked. (Andrewes, 1903, p. 3)

Hold this, then, if you can, for all that remains of the time ahead. Be assured of love, support and prayers in your journey. The road ahead is full of surprises. Sometimes the journey will be exhilarating; at other times it will feel like the proverbial wilderness; and at other times you will wonder why you left Egypt at all, where you were surely better off. But this is not to say that the Promised Land is just around the corner (although our set psalm for today does petition God to 'lead us to your Holy Hill, and to your dwelling').

It is, rather, to say that the Jesus who asks you, 'Who do you say that I am?' also asks, 'And who are you?' The question is ever before us, as we commit ourselves to this calling: to becoming the person, people and place that God is forming us into. If we are faithful, God will surely answer us, 'You are my beloved, my chosen one – the one in whom I delight to go and bear fruit, fruit that will last.' So come, let us walk together, and follow the Lord of the Journey.

Article Eighteen: On Healing Ministry

Ministry to the margins

If I had to be reincarnated as an animal, I would come back as a St Bernard dog. I have my reasons. First, I'd like to be a saint, and this is about as close as I'll get. Second, I believe in searching for the lost. Third, everyone loves a good dog, so there is a chance of being both liked *and* gainfully employed, and you can rarely do *both* of these in the Church. And finally, a rescue mission that involves a flask of something warming can't be all *that* bad. Indeed, find or lose your victim, it still ends with a well-deserved drink.

One of the more famous quotes from another saint of the same era as Bernard is from Benedict: 'Before all things and above all things, care must be taken of the sick; so that the brethren shall minister to them as they would to Christ himself; for he said: 'I was sick and ye visited me' (Rule of St Benedict, Ch. 36). Benedict had read his Gospel: 'Jesus went forth and saw a great multitude and was moved with compassion towards them, and he healed their sick' (Matthew 14.14).

I once published an article on the healing miracles of Jesus which pressed the question not about whether or not these miracles ever happened, but what they meant to their audiences, either as events or as written narratives. It caused a bit of a storm – at least for theology. Friends, and one or two critics, accused me of drafting the gospel according to New Labour. One or two felt it might be the gospel according to Old Labour, but just with a bit of spin.

The paper effectively argued that the healing miracles of Jesus were not in themselves particularly important, either as historical events or as narratives. What was more significant about the miracles were the political implications that flowed from them. I drew attention to the fact that in the 40 or so healing miracles recorded we hardly ever learn the name of the person who is

healed. This seemed to me to be in itself quite significant, pointing to the insignificance of the subject. What was arguably more
revealing about the nature of the miracles was the Gospel-writers'
willingness to tease the reader by naming the category of afflic-
tion: leprosy, mental illness, single mothers with dead children,
orphans, people of other faiths, the elderly, the handicapped.

I could go on. Jesus hardly ever heals his friends, and rarely ever
heals anybody with any significant social or moral political status. In nearly every case, the healings of Jesus are directed towards
those who are self-evidently on the margins of society, or who have
been excluded in one way or another from the centre of social,
political, moral or religious life. Not only that, the friendships that
Jesus made also suggest that he was more than willing to share his
time and abundance with this same group of people.

This observation is not particularly interesting in itself, but it
does start to raise a question about what the healing miracles were
for, if they are in effect 'wasted' on groups of people who appear
to be unable to make a significant response. Yet when one turns
to the sorts of encounters that Jesus has with religious and political authorities, particularly when they are accusing other people of
betrayal (a woman caught in adultery springs to mind; equally, the
prostitute who anoints the feet of Jesus in the middle of a dinner
party, recorded in Luke 7), we begin to see that Jesus' healing activity was, for the authorities, a dangerous, even subversive activity.
Jesus consorts with the *wrong* sorts of people in the eyes of the righ-
teous; he's not in church, but down the pub. Moreover, Jesus gets
no return for his investment in 'the lost' or 'the unclean'; he wilfully loves the loveless, and seeks out those whom everyone else has
given up on. In all of these healing encounters, the remarkable thing
about Jesus' ministry is that it discriminates – *for* the unknown, the
lost, the marginalized and the victimized. And almost nobody else.

For example, in Mark 7.25–30, the Syrophoenecian woman is
one of several people for whom Jesus performs a healing miracle
who do not belong to a Jewish faith community. She is distraught
on account of her daughter. There is no price for her miracle:
she does not have to come to church now. Nor does she have
to become a Jew. No. She simply receives the compassion of
God poured out in Jesus Christ. She's not defiled in Jesus' eyes

at all. Which explains why the stories are linked together. After Jesus' careful lecture on purity, the disciples still want to send this woman away – she's not one of their kind. But she persists.

This is only a brief summary of the article, but you might like to know that it concluded by offering some reflection on the then state of the National Health Service, which at the time was being reshaped by a Conservative government. There was a general attack on the rhetoric of praising and blaming patients for 'their' illnesses, which ranged from exploring the appropriateness of criticizing obese people for eating the wrong foods, to young, single teenage mothers in certain kinds of housing, and social welfare benefit. All very ugly and irksome.

In my conclusion, I simply said that this kind of approach to healing and health care had no place in a modern society, and little place in the Gospels, since the healings of Jesus, although miraculous, nearly always interrogated the *social* causes of dis-ease. That is to say, Jesus was interested not just in healing, but how people had been classed as 'ill' in the first place, and what or who kept them there. He was, I suppose, in modern idiom, tough on illness, and tough on the causes of illness.

We need to remember that when Jesus heals the leper, he makes himself unclean by touching a source of impurity. The radical demand of Jesus is that the Church is required to assume the pain and impurity of the excluded, the demonized and the (allegedly) impure. That's why there are prison chaplains; that's why the Church works *for* and *with* asylum seekers; that's why the Church questions common sense, social control and prevailing political powers. It is just carrying on the job of Jesus, namely looking for the lost, rejected, marginalized and fallen, and trying to, with the love of God, bring them back into the fold of society and the arms of God. Moreover, the Church always asks: 'How did you get here? Who excluded you?' Or, what kind of society is it that *rejects* people – for being too ill or infirm, or the wrong kind of people. Jesus, the friend of tax collectors, prostitutes and other undesirables – but it's not how we like to think of Christ, is it?

But I guess that's the trouble with Christians – we only regard ourselves as honorary sinners, and the Church as a haven for the saved and secure. But it is for the lost and the loveless. In view of this, there are three lessons to learn about Jesus and his healing of the Syrophoenician woman's daughter, and countless others like her.

First, each of the healings seems to indict witnesses, crowds and others who appear to have colluded with the categories of sin and sickness that have demonized individuals and groups. Jesus' healing ministry is decisive in that it questions these categories ('Who told you this person is unclean?' 'He who is without sin may cast the first stone.'). Jesus appears here to be a barrier-breaker, eschewing the normal categories that dumped people in 'sin bins', or constructions of reality where they are deemed to be less than whole or suitable. In effect, he turns the tables on his audience on almost every occasion, and asks in whose interests this person is being categorized as ill or evil. This is why he's crucified in the end; Jesus breaks down the barriers between clean and unclean; he reorders society; the old rules no longer work.

Second, and correspondingly, Jesus often insists that a person returns to the centre of the community from where they were originally excluded. One of the best examples of this is the mentally ill man who has been chained up in a graveyard, and whom nobody visits, recorded in Luke's Gospel. Jesus' healing of this man is extraordinary, precisely because he insists on returning him to the community that expelled him from their midst in the first place. On another occasion, Jesus sends a healed leper back to the people who would have cast him out of the community for his leprosy and uncleanness – and soon everyone knows that the leper is back.

Third, touching is also an extraordinary feature of Jesus' healing ministry in so far as he seems willing and able to take on the associated stain, stigmas and taboos of his society by getting his own body and soul 'dirty'. Social anthropologists like Mary Douglas have had much to say about this and point out, quite rightly, that categories such as 'pollution' and 'cleanliness' surface particularly in relation to our bodies, which she identifies, of course, as a matter of politics. Correspondingly, what flows into and out of bodies, or what is deemed to be 'unclean' and tainting of individuals or communities (such as leprosy), assumes a special character in nearly all societies, from the most primitive to the most sophisticated. Jesus seems to have no fear of touching and healing a woman who is haemorrhaging, of touching lepers, and of generally embracing people whose bodies are leaking sin and pollution, for which they are excluded from mainstream society. He inculcates their stain, blemish and suffering, rendering them whole by embracing their exclusion.

Today, we often forget that visions and missions in virtually every religious tradition in the world are not constructed by disciples or religious groups. They are in fact given – in effect, revelations. These revelations do not offer *choice*, but rather *obedience* in the context of a proper *vocation*. And perhaps our only way forward is to underline the imperative of vocations as an essential fundament in the proper ordering of a humane society. So our task – in our mission – is to look out for today's lepers. To look out for the excluded, the 'impure', the demonized. This is where Jesus will be, always before us. And as the gospel says – he reached out, and he touched. Or perhaps, like our erstwhile St Bernard dog, he searches for lost causes. And he comes with warmth and a drink.

And remember also the words attributed to D. F. Strauss, the nineteenth-century theologian and romantic: Cure Sometimes; Relieve Often; Care Always. So may almighty God bless us and keep us as we dedicate ourselves to his mission, and in the vocations that he has given to each of us.

Part Three: Corporate Religion

Article Nineteen: On Prophetic Gestures

Radical risks for God?

(The Archbishop of York cut up his dog collar live on television in 2007, to protest against the regime of Robert Mugabe, vowing not to wear another until that regime is ended.)

Few remember the name of Jan Palach. His native Czechoslovakia had been invaded by Soviet forces in August 1968, crushing the 'Prague Spring' government of Alexander Dubček. Yes, the world protested, huffing and puffing its way through the countless meetings at the United Nations. But diplomacy, mediation and politics had all failed, and military responses could not be countenanced. Czechoslovakia was on its own. So Palach, a young 21-year-old student, took himself into Wenceslas Square, doused himself with petrol, and lit a match.

His death seemed pointless to some. Yet to others, the act of self-immolation is the ultimate political gesture. So while the sight of the Archbishop of York cutting up his dog collar live on BBC TV to protest against the government of Robert Mugabe is hardly in the same league, it nonetheless stands within a long Old Testament prophetic tradition.

Faced with political corruption or rampant moral turpitude, the prophets of the Old Testament knew exactly how to counter social indolence, apathy or impotence. Ezekiel shaved his hair to symbolize the fate of Jerusalem. He burnt a third, cut up a third, and scattered the remainder to the wind. The prophet Jeremiah engaged in eccentric behaviour, walking about the streets with a yoke around his neck.

But such gestures, while undoubtedly designed to attract attention, are also 'acted parables'. When Dr Sentamu cuts up his dog collar live on television, he sends a message that is more powerful than words. A dog collar is, for any priest, a sign – one that symbolizes service and sacrifice. But it can also signify status and significance. In cutting up his dog collar, Dr Sentamu sends two messages in a single act. First, that cuts are often painful, and that the world should begin to recognize the pain and poverty of Zimbabwe. Second, that his own life and identity as a priest and prelate cannot continue normally while his fellow human beings suffer at the hands of a despotic leader.

The cutting up of a dog collar is, like many gestures from Old Testament prophets, seemingly quirky and eccentric. Yet it sends a deeper, more powerful message: thus far, and no further; the line is drawn here; God will not be mocked; it is time for the world to act. In cutting his dog collar the Archbishop slices through that thin white line of demarcation between priests and people, to stand in solidarity with the oppressed.

Article Twenty: On Remembrance

Fellowship with the fallen

The idea that good may come out of evil, and that self-sacrifice can bring liberation, are two basic paradoxes that lie at the heart of many religions. And one of the stranger things about the month of November is the way in which we are all gathered up into acts of remembrance – All Souls, All Saints – that underline how death can also be the bearer of life, and that light is only truly appreciated when the darkness begins to cover us.

But there is more to remembering than mere recollection. We don't recall events merely to test our memory. The function of memory is much richer. It is something in our processing – our mulling, sifting and the discerning of events – that makes memories richer, not vaguer, as we get older. It is easy to recall things. But memories are what hold, value and discern the significance of what we recall. And as we grow in wisdom – hopefully! – we find new, richer meaning in what we recollect.

Of course, we live in an age of cultural amnesia. It is no better in the Church. The fact that the Church lives in difficult times is not the problem, says the Dutch missiologist Herbert Kraemer. The fact that we constantly forget the Church has always lived in difficult times – that is the problem. This is partly why *remembering* is so vital in our time. In an age of rapid consumerism and short-term solutions, we do well to dwell on what it means to remember, and why this might be important not so much for our past as for our present and future. Of course, remembering is at the heart of the gospel: 'Do this in remembrance of me' are among the last words Jesus utters to his disciples. And 'Lord, remember me when you come into your kingdom' are among the last words uttered to Jesus on the cross.

But remembrance is not merely fond or regretful recollection. It is, rather, a deeper mystery in which the past, present and future become bound up together. When we remember, we *re-member*, in the sense that we re-assemble and recall. We bring out of the past and into the present those people whom we have loved and lost; those whom we still love, yet see no longer; those to whom we owe a debt, yet cannot pay – or thank enough. Re-membering, then, is not merely making sure we don't forget. Re-membering is, rather, the opposite of dis-membering. To dis-member is to take apart; it is a destructive act, pulling apart something that should be held together.

In contrast, re-membering is putting something together that was already a whole, but had come apart. So when the thief says on the cross to Jesus 'remember me ...', he is not trying to jog Jesus' mind. He is instead saying 're-make' me; 're-create' the me that should be together – but this time as the whole person God intends. What might flow from this? Forgiveness is giving up the possibility of a better past. As George Herbert remarked, he who cannot forgive breaks the bridge over which he himself must pass.

Remembrance, then, is not an act that simply brings out memories of the past into the present. It is, rather, an invitation every year to re-make and re-new the world. By recalling, we are asking God to reshape our lives; to be refashioned, remade and redeemed. To be reminded of something is, likewise, not simply to have our memory jogged. To be 're-minded' is to turn our attention back to something we already knew, and gaze at it more attentively, and carefully. Not for nothing does Paul call for us to be transformed by the 'renewing of our minds' (Romans 12.2). To be re-membered as individuals, as a society, as a country and as nations. If we can be 're-minded', we might be re-made, re-membered and re-newed. To come together like this, at Remembrance, in a simple act of worship, and to pray, be silent and recall, is in a real sense to build on the dedication and self-sacrifice of the past – for the present, and for the shaping of our future together, and apart.

Our memories, then, perhaps assume a greater importance at this time of year than at others. For we recall not only acts of heroism and tragedy, but also the unexpected moments that we can't fully explain. Why one lives and another dies; how we managed this or that; what it was like when all seemed to be lost. One of the great services historians have performed for us in recent years is a re-engagement with the ordinary stories of ordinary people, fighting for their lives, colleagues, kinsmen and countries. They are profound in their simplicity.

I think of the British officer caught by a single German officer behind enemy lines on D-Day. But both have to dig a trench together, to avoid the shelling of the British ships off the Normandy coast. They carry on arguing about who will win the war as they dig together, before the British officer is eventually placed into captivity. But by this time, the two have become friends. Or of the young lad who witnessed the murder of 250 civilians in the early days of the purge of Jews from Warsaw – he hid under the corpses of his friends and family, and made his escape at night. Or the British soldier who shot and killed an advancing German at Dunkirk, but then sat there frozen, unable to come to terms with what had happened. He was evacuated by his friends. Or the young American navy doctor at Pearl Harbor, trying to separate a mother from her dead child.

Then there are the numbers. Six million Jews dead; 3 million of them killed not in concentration camps, but in forced marches and massacres. Around 25 million Russians dead, with perhaps more than half killed by their own side. The Blitz visited on London is the equivalent of a 9/11 happening every month for a whole year. Eighty-five per cent of Germany fought against the East; the rest against the West. And the civilians – many, many more died in our two great wars than those in combat. Millions of people were mere collateral damage; the casualties who were the consequence of war. And where is their memorial?

Forgetfulness is the enemy of justice, and the destroyer of lasting peace; the task that beckons on occasions like this is not 'forgive and forget', but 'remember and forgive'. This is true not just of the world wars, but of South Africa, Northern Ireland, Rwanda and other places. For our reconciliation with each other stems from our reconciliation with God. So it is important that we never forget; but equally important that we move and strive to forgive. 'It is only by accepting the past', wrote T. S. Eliot, 'that we can alter its meaning and power.' Yet this is no easy task.

And in the midst of all this, we have our lectionary readings about journeys. Jonah's journey (Jonah 3.1–5, 10) is one that is all about the numbers. God spares the vast majority of innocent people in Nineveh. The book of Jonah ends with God sparing all the people, and many cattle. And God asks Jonah, 'What is that to you?' But God cares about the falling sparrows, the innocent, the potential collateral damage.

Then Mark (1.14–20) has Jesus coming to Galilee, proclaiming the good news – another journey. The breakneck speed at which Jesus calls and gathers his first disciples should not surprise us. Mark's Gospel is the shortest and, to some extent, a kind of short-hand account of Jesus' ministry. It is reasonable to assume that Jesus had much more to say to the crowds than 'repent and believe, for the time is at hand – believe the good news' (1.15). One can imagine long, eloquent sermons, parables and lively exchanges, even from the outset.

So Mark, in summarizing the essence of Jesus' early teaching, is trying to say something about the urgency and immediate impact of the preacher from Galilee. Yet what is so intriguing about Jesus is the range of people he chose to share in this work. In choosing widely, Jesus gives us a foretaste of what the Kingdom will be like and the Church might become: a place both of diversity and unity, and a true home for all. Though many, one body. Re-membered. This is, perhaps, what we need to remember. And it is also what we give thanks for. Remembrance, though it is sometimes born out of tragedy and pain, is also for thanksgiving: Eucharist.

The philosopher Alain de Botton tells us that thanksgiving is part of the fundamental core of faith and religion. One of the differences between religious and secular lives, he says, is that in the former one says 'thank you' all the time: when eating, going to bed, waking up, for this day, for life. But why does the secular world tend not to say thank you? It is possibly because to live in a state of gratitude is also to embrace our human vulnerability. As de Botton says:

> To feel grateful is to allow oneself to sense how much one is at the mercy of events. It is to accept that there may come a point when our extraordinary plans for ourselves have run aground, our horizons have narrowed and we have nothing more opulent

to wonder at than the sight of a bluebell or a clear evening sky. To say thank you for a glass of wine or a piece of cheese is a kind of preparation for death, for the modesty that our dying days will demand.

That's why, even in a secular life, we should make space for some thank yous to no one in particular. A person who remembers to be grateful is more aware of the role of gifts and luck – and so readier to meet with the tragedies that are awaiting us all down the road. (de Botton, 2010)

So, in remembrance and gratitude, we give thanks for God's graciousness. That he numbers the hairs of our head. That he does not forget the fallen sparrow. That God remembers. He cherishes what he knows of us – his creatures, and his creation. Nothing is lost to him.

And so, in our turn, we remember and give thanks too. For all those who have gone before us. For those who gave their lives so we might live. For the costly and sacrificial gifts that have been given; for the yesterdays of others that have enabled our tomorrows. For the souls and saints we cherish; those whom we love yet see no longer.

We remember those who have kept and held us together when we felt we might fall apart. For all those who have re-membered us when we thought we might be dismembered. We do this in remembrance, and with gratitude. In dwelling on the generosity and goodness of God, we remember that we are loved by the God who remembers each and every one of us, and all the hairs of our head. And he looks upon us with gratitude for the love and service we render to one another.

Article Twenty-One: On Blessing and Dedication (Candlemas)

Waiting for God

The best days of Christmas for me are those that fall between 1 January and 2 February, the Feast of Candlemas. Strictly speaking this time has more to do with Epiphany-tide than Christmas, but I like the time because the Christmas story rolls on in quiet, subtle ways that are redolent with anticipation: the fullness of God revealed in Christ. It is all to come, but it has already arrived . . .

Candlemas is a strange festival. Originating back as far as the fifth century, it was a feast for blessing the candles in church, as well as commemorating the encounter of Jesus, Mary and Joseph with Simeon and Anna. It is the last childhood 'snapshot' we have of Jesus. Next time we meet him in the temple as an adolescent, confounding teachers and scribes, and then not again until adulthood. So the childhood stories, packed as they are with meaning and symbolism, are worth unpacking. Even more so, since Candlemas is a 'pivotal feast', one last look over the shoulder at Christmas before the serious season of Lent gets underway. Today, Christmas is over. In our house the crib sets are put away for another year; baby Jesus is wrapped up and stored away; the Wise Men and their exotic beasts of burden put into hibernation; the shepherds put in boxes.

What should we make of the 'odd couple', Simeon and Anna, waiting to see the Holy Family? They are a bit late in getting in their plaudits, aren't they? The shepherds have long gone, and even the Wise Men are on their way home. Yet the gospel carries an important message in stretching out the timeframe for recognizing Jesus. Consider the Wise Men. The genius of their story lies in the fact that they come to Jesus through unconventional routes. They are, if anything, from one of the world's older faiths

(Zoroastrians). They do not get to Jesus by proper observance or by following the Old Testament – they come through their religion to see the light, and, this is important, they return home with it. It is almost as though Luke is finding a way of saying this: 'It does not matter how, where or why you search for the truth . . . as long as you can learn to kneel at the crib.'

Anna and Simeon are apparently more conventional, although their religion is offbeat and marginal even for Luke. But they have both waited, kept their counsel, waited, and waited, and waited. I like their part in this aspect of the Christmas story, for waiting is what many of us must do. But there is an important distinction to be made here: that between waiting and dithering, of being patient and of being delayed. Let me say more.

Many countries have folk tales that rewrite the Christmas story in the vernacular. One of my favourites is Baboushka, a Russian folk tale. In this story, the Wise Men call on Baboushka, a toy-maker, who is busy making toys for selling. They invite Baboushka along to offer a toy to the Christ Child, but she says she is too busy, and sends them on their way. Later she regrets this, and decides to try and find the infant king on her own . . . but she is too late. The Wise Men and the Holy Family have moved on; the legend says that down the ages, you can hear Baboushka calling out for the Christ Child, scouring the land, looking for Jesus to give him her gift. The message is clear: don't delay – hurry to the crib.

Similarly, there is a Catalan Mystery Play dating from the four-teenth century, in which one of the star parts is 'the crapping shepherd'. This poor character, having been visited by the angels and told where to go, is desperate to relieve himself so takes a detour. But his delay is costly, and he misses the Holy Family too. In the staging of the play, he sits centre stage, crouching, with his trousers down at the bottom of his legs – a reminder to folk that nothing should hold us up.

But Anna and Simeon have not rushed. We are a full month on from Christmas. So why are they rewarded? 'Better late than never' is a wise old English proverb, and probably goes some way to answering the question. For the virtues of determination, patience and waiting are rewarded. The tragedies of Baboushka and her Catalan equivalent are not the only side to the Christmas story. Good things also come to those who wait.

And isn't this the point of Candlemas? Part of the genius of the Christmas narrative is to make us journey to see Jesus – we need to go looking for him; seek him out; make an effort. But the gospel also tells it another way. To those who cannot move or do not know, God will also come. Later in the life of Jesus, Jesus will meet seekers, but he will also seek the lost and the ignorant, and those who'd never thought of looking; he is there for them just as much.

Of course, Simeon and Anna are not 'lost'; they bide their time, knowing their moment will come. They dare not leave the temple unless they miss their date with destiny. Others must journey; they must wait. And most of us, I guess, may be somewhere in the middle. Here is a wonderful, humorous rhyme, called the 'Snail Christmas Poem' (original source unknown):

Of Orient there were three snails
Who followed ancient Bedouin trails
To see the birth at Bethlehem
Their names were Nathan, Gar and Shem.
They crept behind the shining star,
The going slow, the distance far
And came just thirteen years too late
(the gospels don't record their fate)
But lucky Nathan, Shem and Gar
Were present at the Bar Mitzvah.

Better late than never: a gospel truth, if ever there was one. And isn't it strange that the last people in the Christmas story are probably the oldest and wisest. Anna and Simeon, who embody the wisdom of waiting, the virtue of patience, and the strength to endure, are rewarded for being there – for not deserting their posts.

The outcome of this encounter at the temple is the beautiful Nunc Dimmitis, still probably most familiar to us in the language of the *Book of Common Prayer*:

Lord, now lettest thou thy servant depart in peace: according to thy word.

For mine eyes have seen thy salvation,
Which thou hast prepared before the face of all people;
To be a light to lighten the Gentiles and to be the glory of thy
people Israel.

According to Luke, Simeon blesses the child and the family, and leaves Anna, whose words are not recorded, to prophesy. To be sure, this is a strange encounter on a special day. Jesus has been brought to the temple to be consecrated as a firstborn male as custom demands. But as with all consecrations, the blessings are multiple. Simeon and Anna are blessed as much as those they came to bless.

And blessing and consecration is what sets our faces forward to Lent and beyond. Blessing, in as far as you can ever define it, is elevating things to their proper place under the gaze of God. Jesus is blessed when he is recognized for who he is. God returns the blessing to those who take the initiative. And consecration? It is simply that act of setting someone or something apart and making it or them 'holy'. Nothing more; nothing less.

Strangely, it is here, in the temple, that Jesus begins his ministry. For here he is truly recognized as a light for both Israel and the world, and is set apart by the faithful witnesses who have waited for him. The road to Calvary begins here: 'the falling and rising of many . . . and a sword shall pierce your own heart'.

Candlemas is a wonderful and appropriate time to be remembering the consecration of Jesus – and another consecrations. It reminds us that the people we set apart for things are never removed from us; holy does not mean separate. It means singled out for a purpose, one in which the light of God's grace can be especially channelled and seen. The light is for the world, not the light shade. Simeon and Anna see this – uniquely – in Jesus. We hope to see a little of it in our bishops. But more seriously, Candlemas is our feast too. The light that Christ bears is to shine in us too; we are, in a sense, the candles to be blessed.

I sometimes think how funny it is that Jesus spent so little time in religious buildings, and on the first two occasions, like most children, he has been taken there by his parents with little choice in the matter. When he was old enough to make up his own mind, he hardly ever seemed to go. But it is good that Luke affirms that Jesus can be found in the temple; this is the manifestation of God. You can find him outside the church – but he has also been known to visit occasionally too. God is not constrained by our walls, whether physical, tribal or doctrinal – and he sometimes gets inside them. Simeon and Anna find God inside faith; many don't.

So Candlemas reminds us that although there is a time to journey and look for God in the big blue yonder, there is also a time just to wait in the spaces of faith and belief – sometimes for a long time. Waiting for God, for the light to come. And come it will. The grey skies and darkness of Lent always give way to the radiant light of Easter. For Simeon and Anna, the light came early – but late in their lives. For others it comes later still. But the light shines. Candlemas says, 'Look – open your eyes, wherever you are, and whatever you're doing – Jesus is here, now.' So, come, enter into the mystery.

Article Twenty-Two: On Thanksgiving

The harvest within

Thanksgiving is central to Christian life. And at harvest time churches give particular thanks for the generosity of God. In Britain, harvest festivals see churches awash with produce – and with accompanying suppers and lunches. And in the USA and Canada, Thanksgiving follows the same vein. Canadians give thanks on the second Sunday of October, and Americans on the fourth Sunday of November. But give thanks for what, exactly? Quite simply, for the good gifts we enjoy. The origins of the Canadian thanksgivings and feasts can almost certainly be traced back to gratitude that marked the end of the harvest season. In the United States, the modern Thanksgiving holiday tradition is commonly traced to a rather poorly documented 1621 celebration at Plymouth in present-day Massachusetts. The 1621 Plymouth feast and thanksgiving was prompted by a good harvest. The custom has evolved to the present, and includes the ritual Presidential pardoning of a token turkey – the rest are not so lucky.

In Britain, it remains the case that harvest festivals mean one thing: churches will be awash with tinned food, packets of cereals and displays of local produce. Improbably large marrows will jostle with baskets of fruit, loaves of bread and sheaves of wheat; brownies, scouts and guides will parade, and clergy will try to say something sensible about harvest festival, a curiously popular service despite the fact that people's connection with food today is mostly with supermarkets and fast-food restaurants rather than the land that provides it.

Although there is a sense in which harvest has always been celebrated (Lammas and Rogationtide come to mind), the modern fondness for the festival is traceable to the Revd Robert Hawker, who, in 1843, building on Saxon and Celtic Christian customs, began to decorate his church at Morwenstow, Cornwall, with home-grown produce. Through the Victorian era, the festival was embellished and romanticized, probably in an effort to counterbalance the influence of the Industrial Revolution and secularization.

However, although the twentieth and twenty-first centuries have seen the observation continue to flourish, the churches' understanding of what, and for whom, the festival is has altered considerably. The *Book of Common Prayer* Collect seems to assume that God is wholly responsible for the weather, and for the abundance of produce; the prayer petitions God accordingly.

In recent times, the festival has shifted in its cultural and theological moorings. Modern collects place little emphasis on God as the fickle conjurer of weather, stressing instead the political and social mandates that issue from a focus on food and provision in a world wracked by inequality and injustice. A prayer used by Christian Aid captures the sentiments well: 'We stand before you, Lord, with hands wide open, ready to receive you . . . our modest gifts, like tiny seeds, not knowing what fruits you may bring out of them . . . asking that our hands and gifts, offered in your service, will make a difference to the world beyond all our imaginings.'

The emphasis has moved from thankfulness for our abundance to one of concern for those whose experience of provision is one of scarcity, or even outright starvation. Harvest festival has, in other words, become slowly, but radically, politicized. This is an important and welcome development, relocating the festival more securely in the cadences of the Old Testament and the Torah. Harvest is a time to consider those on the margins and beyond – those for whom the leftovers, waste and the scraps are enough, or at least necessary.

There is another sense in which harvest is beginning to see its meaning evolve, even if its symbolic forms and liturgies remain apparently unchanged. In thinking about fruits and seeds, and taking a more postmodern turn, it is possible to understand the festival as being something more personal. In sum, the celebration is concerned with the harvest within.

Modern writers of prayers and collects are very much alive to the spiritual aspects of harvest festival and Thanksgiving. In talking about fruit and seeds, offering and growth, life and potential, one can see a simple snapshot that captures the full range of theological shifts in human consciousness.

The God who provides weather and produce (pre-modern); the God who is concerned with the distribution of these resources (political and modern); the God who is concerned with the individual, and his or her inner state or response (postmodern). Increasingly, the cadence reflects the spirit of the age, looking to God the paternal provider; to God as an agent of social and political transformation; and to God as the therapeutic healer, who begins his work deep inside the self, not just deep inside the soil.

This is no bad thing. Ultimately, harvest festival and Thanksgiving calls us to be thankful for what we have been given, acknowledge the giver and, above all, give in return. The quality of the harvest within is judged by what is given out. Some years ago, I read the following advert in my newspaper, which reminded me of the importance of connections in giving, Thanksgiving and harvest:

Why not buy a tree for Africa as your gift to the world this year? For the same £3 a foot you paid for a Christmas tree, you can buy a tree for Hope for Africa . . . which is planting thousands of trees in the [most] fragile areas, providing income and nutrition for local people . . . you could buy a dowadowa tree, which grows to 45 foot. It is known as 'the tree that is blessed by God', because it provides so much . . . its seeds are used to make soumbala balls, a local delicacy that women sell. Young roasted pods make sweets in times of plenty, and are dried in times of famine. Leaves feed the cattle; the twigs make toothpaste; the gum hardens earth floors and can be used to glaze pottery; the flowers treat leprosy; the roots treat epilepsy, and can also be made into strings for musical instruments; the bark is used for tanning, for plastering huts and for embalming – other parts of the tree are used in marriage, childbirth and initiation rituals.

The dowadowa tree is a kind of parable. It suggests that our lives and our work – offered aright to God – can produce an abundant harvest. But it is all about offering and receiving. It is all about looking to the hand of God to feed us, and just as we are fed, looking to others who need feeding, and being prepared to receive from the hands of others.

Article Twenty-Three: On Religion, Nationalism and Consumerism

St George's Day

For many in England, St George's Day (23 April) is little more than an excuse to tarry in the pub, reminiscing over English sporting achievements or heroic failures. For others, the sudden appearance of English flags is an occasion for introspection and doubt. But what about the man behind the flag?

Little is known about St George himself. The details of his life are so scant that he was demoted to the status of a third-class saint by the Roman Catholic Church in the early twentieth century. His fortunes were revived in 2000, when his patronage was recognized as significant. Not only is he the patron saint of England, but also of Georgia, Moscow, Catalonia, Malta, Lithuania, the scout movement, soldiers and skin diseases.

Despite the lack of evidence, the myths of his life have retained their resonance through history. The Christian tradition is that George was probably born in Palestine around AD 260, although his parents are thought to have come from Cappadocia.

He reputedly became a highly regarded cavalry officer in the Roman army, but was tortured and executed during the reign of the Emperor Diocletian in AD 303, after attempting to prevent the persecution of Christians. He was canonized by Pope Gelasius in AD 494. Thereafter, the trail of his hagiology grows cold. A church in Doncaster was dedicated to him in 1061, but otherwise he seems to have received little attention.

He was rediscovered by the military. In 1222, St George's Day became a public holiday. Edward III chose him as the patron saint of the Knights of the Garter, and the Arabic folk tale linked to his name – the slaying of a dragon and the rescue of a damsel in distress – became important ciphers for the early Crusaders, who went into battle sporting the Georgian cross. The idea of rescuing the defenceless and killing the bestial oppressor has inspired many invasion forces.

St George lives on in the English psyche – witness the lines Shakespeare gives Henry V, 'Cry God for Harry! England and St George', and Baden Powell's hymn, which exhorts the listener to 'start out afresh to follow the lead/ Of our patron St George and his spirited steed'.

None the less, most of the mainstream Christian denominations are rather cool about patron saints. This is a pity because they offer a foundation for reclaiming important national, civic and religious virtues often overlooked. Many of the great Christian feasts are not commemorations of actual, historical episodes, bound to specific and verifiable dates. Rather, they are linked to the explanation of religious ideas. For example, no one has the actual date of the first Epiphany, or the first Christmas – but their celebration is linked to the importance of gift and hospitality.

So what might the churches do to redeem St George from lager louts and xenophobic nationalists? One step might be to recognize that the only kinds of sacred time that flourish in a secular era are those spiritual or religious festivals with an explicit link to commercialism. Christmas and Easter have retained their prominence because of the accompanying commerce, not in spite of it. The elevation of Mothering Sunday, and the decline of Whitsun and Ascension Day, prove the point.

Commerce and religion is a powerful alliance. Small wonder, then, that in Catalonia everyone looks forward to St George's Day, as children receive books and women flowers. The task of the churches of England is to do something creative with St George, rather than simply flinching with mild embarrassment. Even if he never existed, his story captures something important: protecting the powerless; standing up to aggressors; sacrifice and sanctity.

Such virtues, wedded to a public holiday, and blended with some nominal commercial customs, could turn a bland, awkward day into a powerful occasion on which the sacred and the secular could come together afresh. For England, and St George.

Article Twenty-Four: On the Unity of the Church

Valuing differences

Just why do churches separate? The old joke about the two fundamentalist pastors shipwrecked on a desert island gets near to the nub of it. When the rescue party arrives, they discover two churches have been built at either end of the island, with both pastors claiming to have founded a new international ministry.

The worldwide Anglican Communion is at present riven by similar tensions. On the surface, the difficulties appear to be centred on issues such as sexuality, gender, the right use of the Bible, and the appropriate interpretation of scripture. These schismatic tendencies in Anglicanism would appear to relate to authority, theology and ecclesial power. But this takes little account of the fact that such tensions have existed within Anglicanism from the outset.

There has not been a single century in which Anglicanism has not wrestled with its identity; by its nature it draws on a variety of competing theological traditions. Its appeal lies in its own distinctive hybridity.

So, another way of reading the current difficulties would be to see them as expressive of the two main competing streams of ecclesial polity that have come together within a single communion. The first is royalist, bound to a culture that is aligned with hierarchy and obedience, and linked to divine right and ordering. The second, which is republican, is essentially democratic in orientation, and therefore about the rights of the people rather than the princes and prelates. Of course, the royalist paradigm for the Anglican Church is not that of an ancient quasi-feudal system, but rather that which emerged out of the seventeenth-century English Civil War, which had deposed notions of outright kingship, but had then restored kingly power, albeit checked by new forms of democratic and parliamentary power.

These two deep cultural streams can be seen as being behind the current, apparently seismic, doctrinal shifts. The election of Gene Robinson (a genial gay clergyman) as Bishop of New Hampshire was an expression of North American faith in the gift of democracy (from God) and the inalienable right to choose. A people who were chosen – liberated, as it were, from the yoke of colonial patrimony – are now called upon by God to continue exercising their God-given rights to choose. The will of a foreign power – or even the mild intervention of a friendly Archbishop of Canterbury – will be seen as an act of hostility and demotic feudalism. The two streams of power, deeply embedded in their respective cultures (not unlike Wilde's notion of two nations divided by a common language) are all it takes to produce two very different kinds of theological grammar within the same communion.

And when such differences are mapped on to the worldwide Anglican Communion, and account is taken of emerging post-colonial identity within developing nations, which are suspicious of both the old ordering of kingly power and the apparent consumerism of the democratic stream, the stage is set for some big divisions to emerge, which will disguise themselves in the terms of doctrinal and ecclesial difference.

Yeats's poem mourned that 'things fall apart, the centre cannot hold'. But the centre was always contested, not settled. So what is to be done? No single solution presents itself. Recognizing that there are cultural factors in shaping and individuating churches is important. Valuing diversity alongside unity will be vital. And praying fervently with Jesus 'that we may all be one' will also be crucial – although one might perhaps mutter in the same breath, 'But thank God we are all different.'

Article Twenty-Five: On the Unity of All the Churches

Valuing diversity

According to Norman Maclean's novel *A River Runs Through It* (1976), a Methodist is basically a Baptist who has been taught to read. This definition is attributed to the Presbyterian minister who features in the novel. But as any Methodist will tell you, a Presbyterian is someone for whom Methodism is a bit too racy. ('Presbyterians', by the way, is an anagram of Britney Spears – although it is not clear how this might please either party.)

These waspish caricatures, amusing though they might be, are symptomatic of a bygone era of interdenominational wars, the kind of which can now only be found in Northern Ireland, Liverpool or Glasgow. For most of the population, religious identity is centred not on the faith of their parents, but on just what happens to be good and local. Ecclesial brand loyalty is a dying phenomenon.

Once upon a time, denominational names mattered a great deal, although their origin is often forgotten. Very few denominations chose their own name. 'Anglicanism' is a term that was popularized by James VI of Scotland, and contains a degree of mocking irony. Similarly, 'Anabaptists' had their family name bestowed upon them by their detractors. Equally, 'Methodist' can also be read as a dubious compliment – another mildly derogatory nickname.

Yet all of these nicknames have eventually been adopted and redeemed by their respective denominational families. Even the curious double-barrelled (and oxymoronic?) 'Roman Catholic' is, in some sense, an externally imposed nomenclature. 'Catholic' should mean universal and comprehensive; but 'Roman' implies imperialist centralization and hegemonic domination.

Religious competition – the very engine of change and growth – fizzled out in the 1950s, and was replaced by ecumenism. The ecumenical movement was meant to find the common ground between denominations as they beat a slow retreat from the rising tide of popular culture, post-war secularization and consumerism. And for a while it worked. The Presbyterians and Congregationalists in England put aside their differences to become the United Reformed Church. Anglicans and Roman Catholics had a dialogue through the Anglican–Roman Catholic International Commission. Methodists and Anglicans almost agreed on unity. Local ecumenical projects flourished.

And yet in the Week of Prayer for Christian Unity, any uninitiated observer might be forgiven for thinking that not much has changed. The ecumenical movement has not yet sighted the promised land of unity. Indeed many churches seem to be specializing in fragmentation and exacerbating their differences. Arguments over gender, sexuality and other issues seem to mock Jesus' prayer 'that they may all be one'.

From my own Anglican perspective, only when the intense heat of the arguments that now bedevil it begins to cool can Anglicanism recover its poise, and its members start talking and listening to one another rather than shouting. The key to Christian unity may lie here, and I suspect other Christian churches are watching with interest. If one denomination can learn to live in humility and grace with its profound differences then there may be hope for a deeper cross-party denominational rapport to develop. Ultimately, unity cannot be imposed: it has to be discovered and cultivated organically.

If the Anglican household of faith can discover a way of keeping itself together with its diversity, it will have made an important contribution to that elusive search for true unity – one that respects the dignity of difference. And in the midst of that, what may also be discovered is that difference is not a sign of weakness, but rather of strength. The diversity within Anglicanism has always been one of its most glorious treasures. It has created the possibility of staying within a faith yet changing, and of moving to and from traditions, yet without abandoning the denomination. Anglicans, like the rest of Christendom, need pray only one prayer this week: 'May we all be one – but thank God we are all different.'

Article Twenty-Six: On Appreciating Differences

Valuing divergence

The late theologian Robert Carroll once quipped that the Anglican way of doing theology was 'the dodo's incorporative principle – a means by which everyone wins'. Anglicans, in trying to sort out doctrinal differences among themselves, were always arguing about the precise weight that should be given to scripture, tradition, reason and culture.

The ground rules for such debates always guaranteed inclusion for participants and most reasonable points of view – even those one might passionately oppose. All sides could always claim a victory, since final decisions were seldom reached. It is precisely this kind of ecclesiology that has made Anglicanism such a rare bird for several centuries.

But is the rarity and novelty of Anglicanism about to slide, rather like the dodo, into extinction? On 15 October (2003), 38 Anglican primates will gather in England to debate homosexuality; prompted by the Jeffrey John affair, the blessing of same-sex unions in New Westminster, Canada, and the election of Gene Robinson as Bishop of New Hampshire, the gathering will explore how Anglican churches around the world can relate to one another, given that the divisions on this issue are now so deep and serious.

There are three possible options. First, there is the carry-on-disagreeing option, though this has had its day. Then there is the option that suggests you divide from those you no longer agree with, and/or expel the heretics. This course is championed by some conservative proponents, but is unlikely to gain much ground because, while hot on certain moral issues, they can be a bit slack on canon law, and do not mind, for example, lay people celebrating holy communion. If moral deviancy is to be punished, what about liturgical or canonical defiance?

Then, there is a third way, which seems to be making some headway. It must be accepted that the worldwide Anglican Communion is really a construction of the empire, though it has evolved into a more equitable commonwealth or federation. It is undoubtedly global, but may now be too diverse to be centrally or collegially governed in a manner that guarantees unequivocal unity.

Overlapping or extended episcopal oversight must be possible in a church that has always valued a degree of pluralism. Geographical boundaries mean less and less; congregations and churches are increasingly related by their shared affinities and agreed moral coherence.

Anglicanism is not, and never has been, one vast, catholic continent. It has always been a kind of archipelago – a connection of provincial islands that shares doctrinal, liturgical and cultural aspects. There are also the virtues of Anglican elasticity and malleability; it is a very adaptive type of church.

It ought to be able to cope with quietly dropping the chimera of communion, and realizing that its identity lies in being more like a family of churches. The Anglican family name could, in future, be used rather like the Baptist family name – the shared essence continues, but the prefix (American, Southern, Reformed, Strict and Particular and so forth) indicates the flavouring.

Whatever the primates decide, my guess is that a degree of separation will not necessarily mean schism, let alone divorce. Indeed, a slight loosening of the ties could help the Anglican churches. Those family members that want the space to be themselves should perhaps be allowed to individuate. Almost 80 million members, in 38 provinces, all living under one roof, might be a bit too stifling for the twenty-first century. So instead of one single monolithic communion, what about developing a neighbourhood or family of Anglican churches?

Instead of trying to patch things up through fear of the unknown, we should try and face the future with faith. Divergence is not a bad quality for churches and denominations. Can Anglicans agree to live a little apart, but still be friends and neighbours?

Article Twenty-Seven: On that Other Issue of Unity

Dealing with disagreement

Canon Jeffrey John was nominated as Bishop of Reading in the Diocese of Oxford in 2003. But after intense campaigning by conservative Evangelicals in the diocese, he was forced to step aside.

Canon Jeffrey John's withdrawal as Bishop of Reading was a major setback for the Church of England, and for the Anglican Communion as a whole. He was, by any standards, an able and suited person for the appointment. He was, moreover, living within the guidelines laid down by the (arguably flawed) 1991 document, *Issues In Human Sexuality*.

But for some, his sexual abstinence was not enough. And in a series of unprecedented manoeuvres, Anglican bishops in England and from abroad united to scupper his consecration. At a stroke, powerful conservative forces have emasculated the historic power of appointment vested in a diocesan bishop, and set back the cause of inclusiveness and tolerance by decades.

I suspect that the victory conservative Christians feel they have chalked up will be pyrrhic. For in pressurizing Dr John to withdraw, the Church of England has failed to take note of the cultural change that has been gathering pace for several years. Instead of presenting a national church able to accommodate gay and lesbian people, it has shown a face of fear, ignorance and prejudice. Such a stance will not woo a nation back to church; it will alienate the young, and baffle all but the most hard-hearted.

To be sure, the 'gay issue' argument is divisive. But it will not ever be settled by one side being vindicated as orthodox, and the other condemned as heretical. Every form of Christianity is an incarnate accommodation of culture; a creature of eternity – but living in time. There is no version of Christianity that is absolutely 'pure', nor has there ever been. Every type and expression of faith has its own local accent and customs. Thus was it always so – even in the New Testament.

There have always been Christians who have been homosexual. They have been a small but significant part of the Church since the beginning. What conservative Christians find problematic is that many more people today want to be more open about their faith and sexuality: they want to be in the Church for who they are, not locked in the vestry closet.

Conservative Christians are also fighting against the world. The tectonic plates of culture have shifted in the post-war era, and homosexuality has moved from being a private vice – for which one could be imprisoned – to being an alternative lifestyle largely accepted in the public sphere. Conservative Christians want to resist culture at this very point, and by taking a stand in the Church, they hope to teach the world a lesson.

But the current climate of tolerance, openness and hospitality is not something that Christians should be trying to reject. Of course, the Bible does encourage the Church to be discerning – Christians are to turn away from sin and error. But the only absolute division that the New Testament ever calls for is between believers and non-believers. And as gay Christians are clearly believers, their sexuality is very much a second-order issue.

Conservative Christians who try to make it a key test of orthodoxy are on dangerous ground. Where will it all end? Going back to excluding remarried divorcees from communion? Ostracizing anyone involved in money-lending? Stoning gay people, as Leviticus demands?

Plainly, the Bible does not speak evenly or unambiguously about sexuality. The few references that may refer to homosexuality – and it is a 'may' – are opaque and problematic. And the texts themselves have a long history of not being consistently interpreted and applied. The Church, too, has a long history of embodying this, mostly by adopting covert double standards.

It is surely time to relocate the debate within more central gospel themes – any who is without sin may cast the first stone; judge not, lest you be judged. These might do for starters. And in the period of quiet reflection that our bishops and tradition rightly call for, Christians may begin to learn to live with their differences.

Article Twenty-Eight: On Disputes More Generally

Christian unity?

It was Jeremy Paxman who once quipped that the Church of England is the kind of body that believed that there was no issue that could not be eventually solved over a cup of tea in the Vicar's study. This waspish compliment directed towards Anglican polity serves to remind us that many regard its ecclesial praxis as being quintessentially peaceable and polite, in which matters never really get too out of hand.

In theological disputes, such as those over the ordination of women, part of the strategy that enables unity can be centred on containing some of the more passionate voices in the debate. Extreme feelings, when voiced, can lead to extreme reactions. And extreme reactions, when allowed full vent, can make situations unstable. Nations fall apart, communions fracture, families divide. Things said briefly in the heat of a moment can cause wounds that may take years to heal. Often, congregational unity in the midst of disputes can only be secured by finding an open, middle way, in which the voices of moderation and tolerance occupy the central ground, enabling the Church to move forwards.

For leaders this means, of course, continually listening to the experiences that lead to anger, and trying to see them from the perspective of those with less power. It means humility on the part of those who hold power, and an acknowledgement of the fear of losing power and control. It means a new way of looking at power relationships that takes the gospel seriously in their equalizing and levelling. I am aware that this is one of the most demanding aspects of oversight, namely having the emotional intelligence, patience and empathy to hold feelings, anger, disappointment and frustration – other people's, as well as your own. Episcopacy, it seems to me, is less about strategy and more about (deeply learnt) poise, especially in holding together competing convictions and trying to resolve deep conflicts.

But before conflicts can be resolved, they must first of all be *held*. And here we find another of the most demanding aspects of oversight within the context of considerable theological and cultural diversity. Because one of the tasks of the Church is to soak up sharp and contested issues, in such a way as to limit and blunt the possibility of deep intra- and interpersonal damage being caused, as well as further dislocation in people's sense of faithful identity. Retaining composure, and somehow holding people together who would otherwise divide (due to the nature of their intense and competing convictions), is a stretching vocation. Anyone exercising a ministry of oversight will understand the costly nature of this vocation. Much of Anglican polity is 'open' in its texture; and although it has a shape, it is nonetheless unresolved and incomplete. Therefore, issues that cannot be determined often require being held; a deliberate postponement of resolution. Put another way, there is a tension between being an identifiable community with creeds and fundaments, and yet also being a body that recognizes that some issues are essentially un-decidable in the Church. Indeed, 'Anglican un-decidability' (a phrase coined by Stephen Pickard, 2012), may turn out to be one of the chief counter-cultural Anglican virtues; it is very far from being a 'leadership problem', as some appear to believe.

The desire and need sometimes to reach provisional settlements that do not achieve closure, is itself part of the deep 'habit of wisdom' that has helped to form Anglican polity down the centuries. It is embodied liturgically in the *Book of Common Prayer*, but can also be traced in pastoral, parish and synodical resolutions that cover a significant range of issues. Essentially, this 'calling' is about inhabiting the gap between vocation, ideals, praxis and action. No neutral or universally affirmed final settlements can be reached on a considerable number of issues within the Church. But provisional settlements have to be reached that allow for the possibility of continuing openness, adjustment and innovation. Inevitably, therefore, any consensus is a slow and painful moment to arrive at, and, even when achieved, will usually involve a degree of provisionality and more open-endedness. This is, of course, a typical Anglican (leadership) habit, embodying a necessary humility and holiness in relation to matters of truth, but without losing sight of the fact that difficult decisions still need to be made.

In summary, we can say that it is partly for this reason that the deep desire for Anglican comprehensiveness is so manifest. To lead a comprehensive church means that it will prioritize conversation and quest over precision and absolute resolutions. In other words, we remain open because we see ourselves as incomplete. This is where our leaders are: holding this vision, to which others continually contribute and compete. This now means, of course, that the centre ground is becoming the radical ground: ironic and oxymoronic, I know – but holding to some kind of centre is, to a large extent, evolving into a task and role that makes the hardest demands upon those charged with oversight. All the more so because, as those who work and study in the field of international conflict resolution remind us, the most difficult and demanding battles are those that involve our own allies or close relationships: what one scholar rather tamely terms 'cooperative disputes'. And such disputes make huge demands on the leadership of the Church. Here we find leaders caught between making moral choices. Do I say what I think, which might be a kind of moral courage? Or do I not say what I think, but keep discussions open – which may be more morally responsible, but runs the risk of being labelled as moral cowardice? Urban Holmes ends his meditation on Anglican polity, written many years ago, with these words:

> It is possible for the Christian to refuse to see the implications of Christ for his or her manner of living. It is a blasphemy to suggest that this is a matter of indifference and the prophet who challenges him is meddling in what is not of his or her business. There is nothing outside God's business. If what the prophet says is not of God, ultimately that is the prophet's problem. God will not be without his witnesses. God speaks and we as Christians must discern what he says to us now, in this place . . .
>
> Ultimately the authenticity of faith and belief is measured at the bar of justice. All religious questions merge into the one query: What shall we do? There is an inevitable course to our

religious profession, which can be aborted only by denying its Lord. That course leads to living in the world as God sees the world. We can debate the trivial points, but the vision is largely clear. To love God is to relieve the burden of all who suffer. The rest is a question of tactics. (Holmes, 1982, p. 95)

Tactics? Can it really come down to tactics? Maybe. But I'd like to suggest that the only tactics that will prevail are those that read the Church and world truly and deeply. They will be those that engage in a rich and profound audit of our ecclesiology and praxis; those that listen intently to the heartbeat of the body of Christ, sounding the depths of the life of the Church. The challenge, then, is clear: to comprehend the real, raw Church in all its complexity, the pain of the world and the pangs of creation, and to work creatively from there.

Article Twenty-Nine: On the Foundations of the Church

Hope for the Church?

Here's an old joke about Anglican polity. One day, the queues of people to get into heaven are so long and thick that the angels guarding the Pearly Gates begin to panic. They fly off to see Jesus and ask for advice. Jesus suggests that potential entrants are graded. He will ask a question of everyone seeking entry, and depending on how they answer, they will either be placed in the slow track or granted immediate entry. The question Jesus proposes to use is the same question he once put to the disciples: 'Who do you say that I am?' The first person Jesus encounters at the gates is a Methodist minister. Jesus asks her, 'Who do you say that I am?' The minister hesitates, and then answers, 'Well, at Conference last year . . .' But Jesus interrupts her immediately. 'I am sorry,' he says, 'but I asked you for your opinion, and not for your denominational line. Would you mind going to the back of the queue? Thank you.' The next person to step forward is a Roman Catholic monk. Jesus poses the same question, to which the monk replies, 'Well, our Pope says . . .' But Jesus again interrupts, and points out that he wanted the monk's opinion, not the Pope's. Third, a Baptist minister approaches. His response to Jesus' question is emphatic: 'The Bible says . . .' But Jesus again interrupts, and reminds the minister that he wanted his opinion, not his knowledge.

Finally, an Anglican priest approaches. Jesus regards the minister somewhat quizzically and with suspicion, but puts the question to him nonetheless. The Anglican replies categorically: 'You are the Christ – the Son of the living God.' Jesus is slightly taken aback by such an ardent response from an episcopalian, and is about to let the Anglican priest in, when the minister adds, 'But then again, on the other hand . . .'.

The first modern *Thesaurus* was published by Dr Peter Mark Roget in 1852, and based on his 'classification of words' – a project he had originally begun in 1805. 'Thesaurus' means 'treasury' or 'storehouse', and if you have cause to use one at all, you will know how invaluable they can be. But what words, I wonder, would Roget have linked to 'Anglican'? It is a potentially awkward question, since the answer will almost certainly depend on the qualities, deficiencies, virtues or vices that the enquirer has already attributed. For some, it will be: indecisive, vacillating or compromised. For others: solid, reliable and predictable. Still for others: conservative – or liberal; historic – or innovative; Protestant – or Catholic.

Interestingly, Roget included 'Anglican' in his original *Thesaurus*, and attributed one comparable word to the term: Protestantism. But then beneath this entry, under 'Anglicism', he suggests another alternative: dialect – a particularly distinctive mode of speech. It is a matter of debate as to whether Anglicanism is a distinctive kind of English Protestantism. It is, and then again it isn't; it is more than that. But Roget's definitions set us a question: what does the word mean?

This is perhaps especially pressing at the moment, but also in relation to today's Gospel. Is the Anglican Communion or Anglican polity 'built on rock' or 'built on sand'? Many will claim the former; some the latter. Some will go further, and say that the sand is quicksand, and we're all being sucked in: by debates on sexuality or gender; by liberalism or neo-conservative fanaticism; by too much attention on the past; or by too much hope being pinned on novel innovations. For some the tradition is solid; for others fluid. And for many of us – and how Anglican is this – neither; something between a solid and a fluid: *flexi-rock*.

The idea that Anglicanism is neither solid nor fluid is not as daft as it sounds. Leaving aside a penchant for the *via media* in all things, the desire and need to sometimes reach 'solid' settlements that do not achieve closure is itself part of the deep 'habit of wisdom' that has helped to form Anglican polity down the centuries. And at the same time, there is enough solidity to prevent the tradition from simply being a form of thick fluidity. Anglicanism, as something in between the two, is a kind of reflexive concreteness;

solid enough for foundations, but sufficiently adaptable and accommodating to be pliable and open.

To my mind, one of the chief virtues of living within a communion is learning to be patient. Churches, each with their own distinctive intra-denominational familial identity, all have to learn how to negotiate the differences they find within themselves. For some churches in recent history, the discovery of such differences – perhaps on matters of authority, praxis or interpretation – has been too much to bear: lines have been drawn in the sand, with the sand itself serving only as a metaphor for the subsequent atomization. Yet where some new (hard, concrete) churches, faced with internal disagreement, have quickly experienced fragmentation, most historic denominations have been reflexive enough to experience little more than a process of elastication: they have been stretched, but they have not broken. This is perhaps inevitable when one considers the global nature of most mainstream historic denominations. Their very expanse will have involved a process of stretching (missiological, hermeneutical, etc.), and this in turn has led directly to their (often inchoate) sense of accommodation.

But to concretize this just a little more, let me offer three brief remarks. First, and in spite of the internal difficulties that global Anglicanism encounters, its strength may still lie in its apparent weaknesses: its unity in its diversity; its coherence in its difference; its shape in its diffusiveness; its hope in a degree of faithful doubt; its energy in passionate coolness. It embodies 'feint conviction'; it practises 'truthful duplicity'; it is Protestant and Catholic; it is synodical and episcopal; it allows for 'troubled commitment'; 'then again, on the other hand . . .'.

Second, maintaining unity in the midst of considerable cultural diversity will lie in developing our poise and capacity to hold together intensely held competing convictions. In the past, this rhetoric of 'holding' has been treated with jocularity or even cynicism by the Church and the public (including the media); it has been a kind of code for saying that no decisions can or will be made (or the bishop doesn't like to make decisions, and prefers to sit on the fence). But increasingly, I think, the language and business of 'holding' will need to come to the fore, and this work and vocation is very far from being vapid or neutral.

Third, we may need to learn to celebrate the gift of our 'un-decidability' a little more. In being able to sustain a community of intense difference and competing convictions, we are offering a form of witness rather than a lack of unity. As the American theologian Urban Holmes notes, 'I have never known two Episcopalians agree totally . . . [but] the fact that we can admit our disagreements is indicative of our Anglican freedom to acknowledge the polymorphous nature of all human knowing – something that not every Christian body is comfortable admitting' (1982, p. 22).

In other words, we remain open because we see ourselves as incomplete; we are constantly caught between innovation and stability; the possibility of new patterns of being, and faithfulness to what has been revealed; between loyalty to what has gone before and still is, and what might or shall be. So, as I return to *Roget's Thesaurus*, I wonder if Anglicans might now be permitted to add words from their own treasury to the label? Solid, yet flexible; strong, yet yielding; open, yet composed; inclusive, yet identifiable.

The list could go on. But I suppose I am appealing for having some confidence in our un-decidability and elasticity, in the very midst of our concreteness. We need both. And at a time when we are being sorely pressed to decide and define instead of living together in patience, we need to have the courage to be, above all, *Anglican*. As I said earlier, we are continually rediscovering the *flexi-rock* nature of our polity – both resistant and accommodating in the expression of our resilience. So in holding the Church together, and keeping it open, we remember that we are, first and foremost, held by God in his open hands, God who knows our weaknesses and differences only too well, but will still cling to us, and not let us go.

Article Thirty: On Women Bishops

Waiting in hope

The failure of the Church of England's General Synod to pass the Measure enabling women bishops in 2012 came as a heavy blow to many inside the Church – but also many outside the Church, who will find the decision hard to fathom. Yet I remain sure that it is only a question of time before the Church of England will take this next step; it is just not now.

A concern for order and unity in the Church is undoubtedly what drives many of those opposing the ordination of women to the episcopate. But a concern for order and unity in all creation – a no less Godly yearning – is just as vital for our Church and world. The Church, meanwhile, must continue to wait prayerfully and hopefully, and in a spirit of charity.

The Church lives constantly in the tension between patience and faithful reform. On the one hand, it is bound to remain true to its given nature. On the other hand, it is bound to reform and change in each generation, as the Holy Spirit continually renews the Church. In a famous if rather overlooked essay written over 60 years ago, Yves Congar, the renowned French theologian addressed the subject of true and false reform in the Church. Congar, a Roman Catholic, was attempting to reach out to the Protestant denominations, and re-engage with the spirit that had given birth to the Reformation. Like all Christians, Congar believed in unity. But he was also realistic about the differences, diversity and disagreements that caused division.

In his essay (1950; translated in 1962), Congar starts with the virtue of patience. He moves on to explore how impatient reform can lead to the reformers believing themselves to be persecuted. And although the essay ends with a plea for unity, and for continued patience and dialogue, Congar's revolutionary insight was that church leaders ultimately have a responsibility to *not* be too patient. In other words, a moment comes when a decision must be made. Hopeful patience may prove to be wise for sometime. But pointless waiting is merely prevarication posturing as discernment.

The Church knows a great deal about waiting. It waits for the coming of the Kingdom. In Advent, it waits for the coming of Christ. In Lent, the Church waits for the radical transformation of Easter. Each of these periods of waiting is hard, yet anticipative, but is neither pointless nor endless.

The Church waits in hope. Because it believes that through waiting, wisdom, discernment and new insight will enable a purer and clearer leading of the Holy Spirit. All Christians know this can be difficult and demanding; but that for a flourishing Church and the mature spiritual life of individuals, it is essential.

In respect of the ordination of women, there has already been much waiting. The earliest campaigners for women's ordination – those on the fringes of the suffragette movement, such as Maude Royden – could barely have imagined that it would have taken more than a century for women to receive equal treatment in the Church of England.

It was 1912 when Royden began editing *Common Cause*, the journal of the National Union of Women's Suffrage Societies. Five years later she became assistant preacher at the City Temple in London – the first woman to occupy this office. After the Great War ended, she founded the Society for the Ministry of Women, campaigning and speaking for the ordination of women well into the 1940s.

Royden did not live to see General Synod passing a motion in 1975 stating 'this Synod considers that there are no fundamental objections to the ordination of women to the priesthood'. And then General Synod, in 1978, asking the Church to 'prepare and bring forward legislation to remove the barriers to the ordination of women to the priesthood and their consecration to the episcopate'.

The first women were ordained to the diaconate in England in 1987. The first women ordained to the priesthood followed soon after in November 1994, with 38 of the Church of England's 44 diocesan synods voting in favour. And for the more recent debates on women in the episcopate, the numbers were even better, with

42 out of 44 dioceses voting in favour of women bishops. Maude Royden, you might think, would be rejoicing in heaven. She will have seen the celebrations of her American cousins taking place many years earlier. The Episcopal Church has had the pleasure and privilege of women bishops for many years.

But some will never move, and it is because of this that the duty of our church leaders not to be too patient now comes more sharply into focus. To place this in context, I have only to recall a conversation with a diocesan bishop opposed to the ordination of women. I asked him about the wider implications of already having women bishops in the Anglican Communion.

What would he do, say, with a male priest who had been faithfully offering priestly ministry overseas for many years, but was ordained by a woman bishop? And if that same priest now asked him for permission to officiate in his diocese when he returned home? Would he grant the licence? No, he said. Would he insist on some sort of conditional re-ordination? No, he said. Then what, I asked? He replied, simply, that he would ordain. There was no question about this: the man was not a priest, and he never had been.

Herein lies the rub. The legislation before Synod was already a 'compromise', in the original sense of that word. That is to say, it was a co-promise: an agreement that together we would move forward mutually, not severally. It was this that the Synod had set its mind to. That the Church lost sight, so early, of a simple one-clause measure, is a real tragedy. And it was this failure of leadership, ultimately, that led the Church inexorably and slowly to the vote's result.

How can the Church of England move forward? As a body, we seem to have been quite slow in learning that diversity, disagreement and difference cannot simply be managed into consensus. The political, synodical or managerial solutions that have been proffered so far have singularly failed to inspire and galvanize most of the debaters. And the public, understandably, have largely switched off in droves.

There needs to be greater trust in the processes of Synod – for God meets us in meetings; and here we find truth too. But what is also needed is better and inspiring theological leadership (not just clearer or louder) that will lift the debate into a different dimension. This was lacking on the floor of the Synod debate. And its more general absence from the Church quickly leads to a rather pedestrian debate about the rights of groups and individuals, how they compete and conflict, and how to find compromise.

The only sure result here is that everyone loses. Indeed, that was the result of the debate: nobody won. The Church lost; the campaigners for women bishops lost; and the apparent victors lost too – but by a margin that gave them the strangest of pyrrhic victories. And the public lost too. They have lost confidence in a church that is supposed to serve the whole nation, and not just the qualms and proclivities of small squabbling interest groups.

What is not needed, I am sure, is for the debate to speedily descend and degenerate into a left–right divisiveness. Some quickly and eagerly talked about the Equality Act and relished the prospect of political interference. Others inferred that the principal problem is falling attendance, with further inferences and accusations of being out of touch with modern values. None of this will work, I fear.

At present, and in our attempts to organize the Church and manage its diversity, we are often guilty of trying to 'give unto thy servants that peace which the world cannot give' to ourselves. But it is a gift of the Spirit, grafted through conversation, conflict and slow consensus that gradually builds us into communion. The genius of Christianity lies in its contestability; therein lies its richness too.

If diversity could have been easily managed, the New Testament would perhaps have given us some pointers; and the apostles and early church Fathers might then have led the way. But alas, it is something of a conceit of modern times to suppose that the Church is an organization in which diversity can be ironed out, difficulties managed, and the Church homogenized into a discourse of uniform clarity for the media and the public at large. The Church is a body that seeks unity in the midst of diversity; it does not aspire to being an ecology of managed uniformity.

Munir Fasheh (1992), the feminist Palestinian theologian, offers a telling insight into how the debate on women in the episcopate is now beginning to feel for all the women (and many men) who long and pray for women bishops in our Church. Fasheh tells of how a woman in Beit Sahour (near Bethlehem) behaved when

Israeli taxation officers came to town. When the army had already taken nearly everything from her house, she finally protested at the removal of her fridge – the last thing left in her kitchen. She said to the officer, 'Why don't you leave the fridge – I need it to feed my hungry children, and the food and milk will rot outside.' Trying to tempt her, the officer said, 'OK – but pay $25, and you can have it.' She said, 'I am not bargaining with you; I am appealing to you as a human being who probably has children.' He said, 'All right, pay $5.' She said, 'You don't seem to understand.' He said, 'OK, pay just $1.' She said, 'Take the fridge – it's yours.'

From the outset, this debate has always been between those charged with a duty to compromise and another group, who, we are told, simply cannot move. But this dynamic has reduced the debate to some kind of plea-bargaining for women bishops. It is humiliating to have to barter and beg. Love, integrity and dignity become diminished when having to bargain for something offered so begrudgingly.

This story from the Palestinian–Israeli conflict is, of course, not a comparable analogy for the debates that currently divide our Church. Our saga is not about the oppressed and the oppressor. Yet the story from Beit Sahour more than does its job in conveying a deep and underlying dis-ease: that visceral sense of bewilderment and betrayal that many women now feel within the Church. After all, pay a dollar, and you get the fridge: a bargain, surely? But as many have discovered before, power gained 'at any price' (whether high or seemingly very low), usually translates into ashes, not riches. So, that proverbial million-dollar question hangs in the balance: can the women bishops' legislation now get through? But Synod is not actually facing a million-dollar question at all. This is a simple one-dollar question, straight from Beit Sahour. Should any gift that is not offered to the Church – fully, freely and graciously – really be bargained for?

The only way forward is for the Church to be, as the apostle once remarked, 'transformed by the renewal of our minds' (Romans 12.2). Here, the word 'renewal' can be taken in at least three senses: a recovery of something lost; improvement of what is in the present; or a complete exchange of the past and present for a new future. Just what kind of renewal the Church of England both seeks and needs is the key to the future of this debate. For this, we need outstanding theological leadership, not a mere suite of managed compromises. And yes, more waiting: but perhaps in hope?

Article Thirty-One: On Richard Hooker and Participation in Christ

God's places of meeting

A 'celebration' of Richard Hooker (on his day, 3 November) – in typical English style, we tend to call them 'commemorations' – reminds me of a story about a Cambridge college that found itself in a dilemma. One of its founders, Bishop John Fisher, was canonised by the Pope about 80 years ago. All very nice you might think, except that the then Master of the college, and most of the Fellows at that time, were staunch atheists. How then to mark the occasion? The answer was beautifully simple: a few lines were printed in the *College Magazine*, under 'News of Old Members'.

Richard Hooker would be doubtless surprised to see himself commemorated in his own right as a 'founder' of Anglicanism on 3 November. His theology is generally regarded as seminal for the development of a distinctively Anglican point of view, but his writings are more often mentioned in allusions rather than discussed in detail. This is partly because Hooker wrote in an unusual style that is difficult for most modern readers to follow. Take, for example, the opening sentence of the Preface to his *Of the Laws of Ecclesiastical Polity*:

> Though for no other cause, yet for this; that posteritie may know we have not loosely through silence permitted things to passe away as in a dreame, there shall be for men's information extant thus much concerning the present state of the Church of God established amongst us, and their carefull endevour which woulde have upheld the same.

As one recent commentator notes (W. B. Patterson, 2000, p. ix), could anything be further from the breezy, often terse, sometimes pungent language of the public intellectuals we read in books and magazines or hear on television?

Hooker's brooding, deliberative, seemingly indirect approach is part of his message. Some subjects need to be examined thoroughly in the light of history and practical use, to be prayed over, and to be treated in a way that recognizes their complexity. This is the way Hooker dealt with issues raised by members of the Puritan movement in England concerning the Church of England. In any case, Hooker's major work, which he presented in this disarming manner, was part of a campaign to oppose them.

For Hooker, God is not the private property of the elect or the faithful: God and God's law are reflected everywhere. This principle has practical consequences. Hooker's teaching is in opposition to all efforts to deny or condemn 'the sensate, the animate, or the inanimate'. For Hooker, the true Christian tradition is 'not world-denying but world-affirming'.

The Eucharist is the 'sacrament of continuing sanctification', by which, in Christ and fed by Christ, Christians grow towards maturity. Both sacraments work within the context of the community of faith. That community is not just the local congregation but the whole Church on earth and the communion of saints. In earth and in heaven the members of the body of Christ assist in this process by their prayers. Regarding Christ's presence in the Eucharist and the transformation the Eucharist brings, Hooker speaks not of the effect of the Eucharist on the bread and wine but on the people gathered for worship.

The purpose of the Eucharist, in other words, is not so much to change the material substance of bread and wine but to change human beings, to bring them together in union with the living God, and to effect communion with God and among themselves. The elements are the means Christ chose to effect this union. They are not mere signs.

Hooker taught that 'we are not to doubt but they reallie give what they promise, and are what they signifie' (Laws, 5.57.5). They not only proclaim that God extends his grace to human beings, but what kind of grace he gives, namely, the nourishment they need to sustain their new lives in Christ. The change the Eucharist effects in the communicants is described by Hooker as 'a true change both of soule and bodie, an alteration from death to life' (*Laws*, 5.67.1 1).

Hooker traced his teaching back to the ancient Fathers of the Church as well as to the scriptures. He called the Eucharist 'reall participation', whereby worshippers receive the whole Christ in a way that brings not only forgiveness but strength and renewal. This is, as I point out in my little *Introduction* to Hooker (Percy, 1999), a Eucharistic theology that transcends the stale controversies over the manner of Christ's presence and restores the conception of the Eucharist as a dynamic action leading to a fuller experience of life in Christ.

Hooker understood that a genuinely catholic Church would be innovative. He had little time for Puritans who would not countenance anything that was not enshrined in scripture. I'm always fond of the quote, taken from Samuel Owen, refuting Puritanism and its attitude to scripture, by accusing Puritans of reducing the Bible to being 'no better than Balaam's ass'. Equally, Hooker was set against a kind of traditionalism that prevented the Church adapting. Substantial parts of Book 5 are taken up with apparently trivial matters – the attire of ministers, music in church, architecture and the manner for administering sacraments. Yet for Hooker, these concerns arise directly out of his conviction that the Church, in its doctrine, preaching, practice and teaching, has some degree of leeway for adapting culturally and temporally. It was obvious to Hooker that church polity need not be *in* scripture, as much as it was obvious to him that it must not be *against* it. Thus, he writes:

> Seeing therefore those canons do bind as they are edicts of nature, which the Jews observing as yet unwritten, and thereby framing such church orders as in their law were not prescribed, are not withstanding in that respect unculpable: it followeth that sundry things may be lawfully done in the Church, so as they be not done against the Scripture, although no Scripture do command them, but the Church only following the light of reason, judge them to be in discretion meet. (*Laws* 3.7.2)

The authority given to reason here is not the elevation of rationality so much as the recognition of the place of common sense. It may well be that certain aspects of the life of the Church do not occur in the New Testament. But their absence does not invalidate their efficacy, since the laws of God (which are for goodness) are part of an ongoing organic church that is imbued with the presence of God. Sometimes God meets us in plain common sense!

In Book 5, the vision of God – which underpins all laws – begins to mature in the various descriptions of the sacraments and the general conduct of ecclesial life:

> Sacraments are the powerful instruments of God to eternal life. For as our natural life consisteth in the union of the body with the soul; so our life supernatural in the union of the soul with God. And forasmuch as there is no union of God with man without that mean between both which is both, it seemeth requisite that we first consider how God is in Christ, then how Christ is in us, and how the sacraments do serve to make us partakers of Christ. (*Laws* 5.50.3)

Thus, in the specific case of the Eucharist:

> The bread and cup are his body and blood because they are causes instrumental upon the receipt whereof the participation of his body and blood ensueth. For that which produceth any certain effect is not vainly nor improperly said to be that very effect whereunto it tendeth. Every cause is in the effect which groweth from it. Our souls and bodies quickened to eternal life are effects the cause whereof is the Person of Christ, his body and his blood are the true well-spring out of which this life floweth. (*Laws* 5.67.5)

For Hooker, the ultimate location of the presence of Christ's body and blood is not to be sought in the sacrament, but rather 'in the worthy receiver . . . only in the very heart and soul of him which receiveth him'. This might appear to be rather bland at first sight, but it is far from that. The key to Hooker's sacramental theology lies not in the minutiae of the Reformation debates about the real presence, but rather in the essence of 'participation', which he calls 'the fruit of the Eucharist'. This participation flows from his dynamic and organic ecclesiology. For Hooker, participation is not over-prescribed or narrow, but is rather public and corporate, and is the key to individual and social life intricately wrapped within the life of God.

And if God meets us in such a broad and generous way, what might our response be? Hooker has the last word, using a phrase that resonates with his warning in the Preface that 'our safest eloquence concerning him is our silence':

> He which hath said of the one sacrament (*i.e., baptism*), 'wash and clean', hath said concerning the other likewise (*i.e., the Eucharist*), 'eat and live' . . . Let it therefore be sufficient for me presenting myself at the Lord's table to know that what there I receive from him, without searching or inquiring of the manner how Christ performeth his promise; let disputes and questions, enemies to piety . . . let them take their rest. (*Laws* 5.67.12)

Here, Hooker reveals himself as an explicit conciliator, offering a vision of genuinely inclusive church. As a form of apologetics, it is a model for all those who seek to hold together competing convictions, and seek to promote unity in the face of polarization. For Hooker knew that God will meet us in bread and wine, and the waters of baptism, and even in our feverish disagreements about how to read and understand the scriptures. For all can participate in Christ.

Part Four: Miscellaneous People

Article Thirty-Two: On St Columba

Sketching the Church

Readings: Titus 2.1–15 and Mark 4.35–39.

There is a story about a Yorkshire clergyman that goes something like this. After years of faithful service to his parish, the time finally comes for him to move on. He calls the churchwardens round to tell them, asks them what they think. But they say nothing, apart from: 'It's your decision, Vicar.' The vicar is a little hurt by this, for they neither say 'please don't go' or 'good luck in your new post'. Indeed, they do not even say 'thank God, and good riddance'. This has never been, rues the vicar, a congregation to wear its heart on its sleeve, and show its appreciation. The vicar duly turns up for his last Sunday, and preaches a most moving sermon. But there is no farewell; no gift and no real recognition that he is leaving.

Imagine his surprise, then, when a year later he receives an invitation to return to his old parish and preach. As he arrives he is shaken warmly by the hand by churchwardens, PCC members (Vestry), and almost all the congregation. He preaches; and the congregation laughs at his jokes – all of them. When the sermon ends, the congregation breaks into spontaneous and appreciative applause. And at the end of the sermon, he is ushered into the church hall, where a lavish spread is laid out for lunch. Speeches and presentations are made, and the old vicar is quite overcome. He turns to his former churchwarden and says: 'In all my time here, you never showed me any appreciation, and now all this – why?' 'Well,' said the churchwarden, 'when we had you here, we always said "We could do worse, I suppose" – and now we have.'

I like this joke because it captures something quintessential about Yorkshire, but also about Englishness. It's what Kate Fox describes in her book *Watching the English* (2004) as Eeyorishness – her word for mild moaning and an unerring capacity for understatement. 'Mustn't grumble'; 'OK, I suppose'; 'could do worse';

'curates' egg'; 'all things in moderation' are part of the national canon of our most cherished casual phrases. It's as though passion and excess were some kind of nasty continental disease that you might get on holiday – a rash, as it were, to be treated with cream.

It is not difficult to be humorous about the modest and temperate proclivities of Anglicanism. Many are aware of the spoof *Laodicean Hymnal* that has recently been proposed for Anglican congregations. 'This collection of hymns really captures the essence of our tradition', states the blurb: 'At the core of our belief is the motto, "Moderation in all things".' The partial list of re-worked titles includes: Not My Life – Let Me Be; Onward, Christian Reservists; Sit Up, Sit up for Jesus; A Comfy Mattress Is Our God; Oh, for a Couple of Tongues to Sing; Amazing Grace, How Interesting the Sound; Pillow of Ages, Fluffed for Me; All Hail the Influence of Jesus' Name!; Be Thou My Hobby. (You can spend the rest of the sermon writing your own.)

Anglicanism, as you probably realize, rather plays up to all this. It is a relaxed, mild, temperate form of ecclesial polity, not easily given to extremes. Rather like the climate of the nation that gave birth to its national church, it is often overcast, but also occasionally sunny; mild, with warm spells. We imagine meteorological extremes, but they are, in reality, merely trifles. As Bill Bryson (1995) observes in his *Notes from a Small Island*, the world giggles when our newspapers have headlines like 'Phew, what a Scorcher', or more risibly, 'Britain sizzles in the 70s'. In most parts of America and the Continent, that is a cue to fetch the cardigan – not strip off and sit down with a 99, plus a flake.

One of my predecessors at Cuddesdon used to describe Anglican polity as a matter of 'passionate coolness'. I rather like this stylistic interpretation of the Anglican mood, since it suggests an actual energy for temperate ecclesial climes. But it has a weakness too, which is that people can often dwell on the actual comfort that accommodation and restraint bring. And such traits can become overrated virtues, if they are allowed to dictate moderation and exclude the excess of passion. If they set the tempo all the time, then the radical of excess, which drives religion, is inhibited.

One of the characteristics that marks out the early Christian saints – one thinks of Columba (almost any of them, in fact) – is that they understood faith to be passion. Faith, in terms of discipleship, is often not reasoned coolness. It is passion that spills over; the love that is stronger than death. It might be thought through. It may even be willed reason. But, my God, it has to be willed with the very fibre of your being. I mention this because it is sometimes easy to misunderstand the place of religion in the modern world, and for people of faith to collude – unintentionally, and sometimes naively – with secular reasoning.

For example, excessive, passionate faith is not the same as extreme faith. The former is intemperate and immodest; but it abounds in energy and love because it springs from the liberty of God. It is released as a kind of raw energy, precisely because it breaks the chains of inhibition, and springs forth from spiritual encounters that can border on ecstasy. But this is not, as I say, extremism. It is merely passion resulting from encounter, conversion, conviction, resurrection and transformation.

Or then again, think about how the Enlightenment and the legacy of modernity has made religion into some kind of 'subject' that is essentially apart from 'ordinary' life. It is as though religion is specious, atypical and abnormal. We talk all too easily of people having 'a religious experience', as though all the other kinds of experiences were 'normal'. But if you turn the phrase around for the moment, you might ask yourself what might it mean to have a 'secular experience'? It would be an odd phrase to use – even in conversation with an atheist. Yet most religious people have accepted the goalposts being moved all too easily. Religions have allowed themselves to be marginalized and particularized, and have even naively participated in the progressive programme of modernity's de-normalization. Religious passion, then, is often narrated as extremism – in most newspapers, TV news reports, and the like. Under such conditions, restraint quickly becomes a virtue that services the controlling of religion: 'all things in moderation', as the English say.

But I'd like to suggest that this understanding of modest, cool faith is potentially problematic. A faith of formation is not adopting a code of control from without. It is, rather, the deep spiritual exercise of restraint for the sake of the self and the other. And, it is a spiritual discipline and a virtue that can only be exercised in proportion to the energy and passion that wells up from the same source. It is not a dainty refusal to take an extra portion. It is, rather, a steely and willed act of moderation or self-control that emerges out of passionate convictions, grace and love.

In terms of Christian discipleship, these observations are important for several reasons. First, passion is not just about the expulsion of energy. It also has another meaning in religion which is concerned with the absorption of pain, sacrifice and suffering – like the passion of Christ. Here, passion is absolutely for the other; but it is passion that is almost entirely configured in its receptivity. Much like the passion of a parent or a lover, God's passion is sometimes spoken in eloquent silence; in sacrifice and in endurance; in solidarity and in suffering.

Second, it is perhaps important to remember that the example of the saints – those people who inspire us in our faith – is often to be found in the delicate combination of passion, practice and reason. You might be surprised at this, but one of the qualities I sometimes look for in ordinands is the inability to contain their passion – for the Church, for Christ and for others. Discipleship is not about being liberal, conservative, or even somewhere in the middle. It is knowing your place before God; being passionate for the possibility of the Kingdom.

Third, the spiritual tempo we seek – which is good and rightful for social ordering and ecclesial polity – should not be allowed to blunt the energy and enthusiasm that flows from living the gospel. To be sure, orderedness and calculation have their place. But an excess of energy must also have its place, even as it risks being narrated as extremism. But religion, of course, is about extremes – extreme love, extreme sacrifice, and extreme selflessness that go beyond reason. Religion in moderation is, arguably, a contradiction in terms. It should offend, cajole, probe and interrogate, as much as it invites and warms.

Saints like Columba show the way here. They are not saints because of their moderation, but for their excess. They are saints because they understood that the gospel is power, it is foolishness, it is offence. It is, in its purest form, a radical expression of the intemperate – God's radical risk in Christ; a love that is stronger than death; a passion and zeal for the other that is beyond manners or common sense. These are the base instincts and desires that drive our vocations. And it is sobering to remember that it is sometimes good and right to encounter them in their rawness, rather than to sift them through the process of formation.

This is why the language of the Bible is so stark at this point. The manna that rains down from heaven does not drizzle – it rains. The Lord appears in a dazzling cloud, and in fire. The message of the New Testament is 'make a choice' for Christ; it is not 'suck it and see'. Our call, then, is to consider the radical nature of commitment, and to call others to this radical discipleship. This is a faith that revels in the excessive, but is not extreme. It is passionate, and yet com-passionately held in such a way as to be persuasive rather than repellent. It is, in short, worth selling the shirt from your back for. Worth it all, and worth sharing.

It can be, therefore, a most intemperate affair. And to have the heart set on God at this point is wisdom. Yes, choose wisdom, and follow him who calls us. This is not to a life where ordinary desires are fulfilled, or even restrained. It is better than that. This is the place where the restless heart is set at ease. It is a place where passion burns as love for the other. The gospel is already a beacon for the world. My prayer for all of you who are to be ordained is: be kind, be good, and be brave – you have nothing to fear. And I pray also that you will continually rediscover the passion and love that drove you to offer yourself – for others, and to God.

Article Thirty-Three: On St Barnabas

Courage and encouragement

Readings: Acts 11.19–end and John 15.12–17.

I managed a wry smile the other day, when one of those surveys was published in a daily newspaper. It concerned the state of school pupils' knowledge of literature. Apparently, children know a lot more about television than books, so much so that this forms the fundamental basis for their archive of memorable quotations. So, while few seemed to know where 'friends, Romans, countrymen' comes from – (*Up Pompeii*, I thought, but apparently it is Shakespeare) – most pupils can recite the pithy wisdom of David Brent, the eponymous hero of *The Office*. One of his quotes is this: 'Just accept that in life, some days you are the statue; on other days, you are the pigeon.' Wise words, indeed, especially as you prepare for public ministry.

Today's Gospel concludes with one of the more memorable quotes from scripture: 'love one another as I have loved you.' Spending much of my life, as I often do, reading essays and theses, I am continually struck by the declining standards in English language. But don't worry, this is not going to be a rant about how things used to be or could be. I am simply opening up in this way to make a point about how vital it is to pay attention to details, particularly in texts. And also to say something about the value of learning to read between the lines.

I mention this all for one simple reason. We often read texts – sacred and secular – through the sieves or lenses that others have bequeathed to us. We rarely stop to question whether the text, read freshly and without overlaying interpretations and modifications, can mean something other than what everyone else once assumed it to mean. Such problems don't merely occur in religious traditions. You can find plenty of examples in various professions, or in the business of statecraft.

And we face this problem squarely with this text. It is arguably the greatest commission we have from Jesus: we are told we are his friends; and we are called to follow his example. Granted, other words from Jesus might just as easily make a claim to be the great commission. What about 'love your neighbour as yourself'? Or 'turn the other cheek'? Or 'whatever you do for the least of these, you do also for me'? To put this more personally, and to put it to you: what is *your* Great Commission? What sends you out into the world, with hope and joy, and a mission to transform it?

The Christian faith contains a number of competitive theories as to what its main priorities should be. But there is a common thread that runs through them all, and it is this. Out of the ashes of Good Friday, of failure, defeat and tragedy, hope and new life are born. And the disciples are to be the ambassadors of the new hope and transformation that is wrought in the person of Jesus. And this role is one that is primarily predicated on developing a dynamic sense of vocation. The resurrection, in other words, is something that does not draw disciples so much into a new sect, as it sends them out into the world, with joy, conviction and a desire to serve the needs of others in the name of the living Christ. And critically, this is done in love: it is not a task; it is an entire reconfiguration of one's life. You see, you cannot really command people to love. That's the catch. Love is for falling into. It is a state of being, as well as doing.

All of us who work in the Church are faced, daily, with a simple dilemma. How do we begin to complete and apply the task that our forebears bequeathed us? How do we bring resurrection and transformation to the base materials, situations and people that we are here to serve? How do we heal the sick, comfort the lost, illuminate the confused; bring hope, joy, peace and wisdom to those who are searching for or needing health and completeness? Be a father to the needy? Help the lame to walk? Be eyes for the blind? Or love another?

Though he is not named among the twelve apostles, Barnabas is clearly one of the leading figures of the early New Testament church. His name is associated with provision, love, leadership and encouragement; indeed, he is the patron saint of encouragement. And if you remember nothing else from this sermon today, then I urge you never to underestimate the power of encouragement. Not just words of encouragement, either, but deeds. Manifest words and ways of saying 'well done', 'keep going' and 'thank God for you'. Barnabas practised encouragement in word and deed; Paul testifies to his words, but we also know that he sold his whole estate to help kick start that unique and 'still-work-in-progress' project we now know as 'the Church'. A Levite from Cyprus, he was martyred in AD 61 – after a tireless and itinerant ministry.

So what of love, provision, leadership and encouragement? Especially as we prepare to bid 'fare well' to those leaving college, and begin the perennial task of re-forming our community; making new space for hospitality, learning, love and growth – even as we still ache from the parting that we must face each and every year.

I think the answer to this is that it is more than you can ask or desire. And that God doesn't waste anything either – even the apparently weak, foolish and fallible parts of our lives he seems to find a use for – and makes do with these abundantly. God does not mind what kind of material he works with, as long as it is supple. In other words, open to being used. We see this in Jesus too. Even in the resurrection – arguably an overwhelming demonstration of God's abundant power over life and death – Jesus returns bearing his scars. The wounds survive the resurrection, because God's wisdom and abundance is sufficient even to speak through the searing pain and reminder of Good Friday.

Our God is an economic God: he uses the weak, the foolish, the scars, the leftovers, the failures . . . nothing is waste to God. Barnabas, our patron saint of encouragement, would have easily understood this. He would know, instinctively, I think, that everything, when it is in God's hands, be it bread and fish, or my apparent failures or manifest weaknesses and shortcomings, are capable of being transformed.

And that is my point. God works through our strengths and weaknesses. This is part of what it means to try and cope with his abundance. He can even use our imperfections for his glory. Clever stuff. You might be wondering why I am prattling on about weakness and failure just at the point when we are about to focus on the concentrated blessing that is poured forth in ordination. But I guess that is my point. One of the artful things that is asked of us in ministry is not only to check on what is going well, and what God is doing in that – but on what is not going so well and what God is doing in that too.

This sometimes requires a special wisdom: to see what God can do with the dark (because it is not darkness to him), and also weakness (which of course he loves to use, to shame the wisdom of the wise). What looks like failure to the world is merely an opportunity for God, a hairline crack or gaping hole through which abundant life and grace can pour.

Barnabas, of course, would be no stranger to these sentiments. He worked well with Paul – but also parted from him in the end. But out of that wound of separation and failure came the evangelization of Cyprus. Nothing is wasted, you see. You can hear the words of Julian of Norwich speaking through to us here: 'All shall be well, all shall be well: and all manner of things shall be well.' Barnabas, as an encourager, would say that you cannot go far wrong if you give it all to God. He'll even use your failures and pain. So please, just hand it over. Don't be shy. He can see it already, and he is waiting to use it.

So let me encourage you. If we are rooted in God, our ministries will become safe places that can afford some risks – maternal and paternal spaces that can cope with pain and some failure. As one writer, John Macmurray (1970), puts it:

> it is often necessary to make a distinction between real and illusory religion. The maxim of illusory religion runs: 'Fear not; trust in God and he will see that none of these things you fear will happen to you.' But that of real religion is quite contrary: 'Fear not; the things you are afraid of are quite likely to happen to you; but they are nothing to be afraid of.'

So let me encourage you. And have courage. It will turn out fine if you are turned over to God. All you need to do is give back some of the love that has already been shown to you. Love is the lesson. As William Langland puts it in *The Vision of Piers Plowman* (c. 1370):

'Counseilleth me, Kynde', quod I, 'what craft be beste to lerne?'

'Lerne to love,' quod Kynde, 'and leef alle othere.'

Just as our Gospel today says, unequivocally, 'love one another as I have loved you . . . you did not choose me, but I chose you. And I appointed you to go and bear fruit; fruit that will last . . . I am giving you these commands, so you may love one another' (John 15.12–17).

So let me encourage you. There is nothing you can do that will make God love you any less or any more. God's love for you is complete, abundant and overwhelming. The mystics say that even God has one flaw – a frailty from which grace flows, which will teach us all we need to know about power made perfect in weakness. God's heart is too soft. And it is from his open heart that we learn about his open hands and embrace. So no matter where you end up in the Church – no matter what mistakes are made, or for that matter, success achieved – remember that in this place you have been loved and cherished for who you are and what you are becoming. That will not change either. We are always here for you; a safe place to be. A seminary. That seedbed in which you have already flourished and flowered, and through which and in you God will undoubtedly bear much fruit. God be with you. And our love goes with you too as you step into the future he is already making for you.

God loves you and has called you to share and proclaim that love. So you have every reason to have courage and to be encouraged.

Article Thirty-Four: On St Matthew

Wisdom and enlightenment

Readings: Proverbs 3.1–6 and Matthew 9.9–13.

It is particularly appropriate, I guess, that we celebrate St Matthew this evening – one calling among many in the Gospels, but a calling that required him to set aside what he had been doing and to follow Christ. The Gospels do not say much about his life and death, bothering only to list his profession – the much-despised tax collecting – but a job that probably made him literate in Greek, Latin, Aramaic and Hebrew. It is not known whether his booth was alarm-protected, or even if the tax-collecting Matthew was the same as the Gospel-writing one. But we know Matthew was called, since all disciples and apostles have to spend their lives figuring out the meaning and intention of those two truly profound words uttered to Matthew, and to all who are called. Simply, 'Follow me'.

So what are we to make of our readings? Of the pursuit of wisdom, or veiling and unveiling, seeing and not seeing; and of course, following? George Fox, one of the early and best-known leaders of Quakerism, instructed his followers to 'turn within to meet the light . . . and then wait in that which is pure'. This might seem like strange advice at the start of an academic year, and perhaps at the commencement of your theological training and formation. After all, you might feel you have waited long enough. Eager to get on, get through, and then get out – 'wait' seems like an odd message to dwell on. Yet the secret of formation, as Fox knew, is to allow the cultivation of inward journeying, personal growth and transformation. And this requires a stillness to accompany the eagerness. To move on with God, and to go deeper, requires a listening and a certain kind of openness. To follow, we have to stop and be still, and listen. To accept that now we have got to this stage – whether just starting, or now preparing to leave . . . or somewhere in the middle – God will start afresh with us.

There is no formula for this. It is not something to be 'done', 'achieved' or 'made to happen'. It is, rather, something about being in the waiting. Understanding that as we prepare for the year, we also let our hearts become prepared – letting God work through the quality of illumination that comes through listening and patient attention to his calling of us. Following Christ is a constant act; a life given daily; not merely one moment or decision.

Of course, the beginning of a journey like this requires us to be open on many levels. For example, consider how God might teach you. For he does not speak only through the wise and intelligent. Sometimes God speaks to us through people far less intelligent than we are, in order to remind us that the weak and foolish things of the world can often be his lively oracles. So if God can speak through Balaam's ass (Numbers 22.28) he might be able to say something to you through a parishioner whose opinion you might not normally seek – or even a fellow student that you wouldn't normally consider your equal. Listening to the voice of God requires humility and openness on our part – we do not know from whom or where he will say something.

In some respects, this is why one of the most important things to focus on while you are at college is not just the study but prayer and worship, and following the one who calls us. In other words, developing a state that moves through partitioning and into integration. Because this really is about following Jesus. And that requires a bit of de-cluttering on our part, and a real willingness, like Matthew, to put up the Captain Lawrence 'Titus' Oates sign, 'I am just going out – I may be some time', on the proverbial booth, and to follow. But for this, you need not just determination, but also a good heart.

Theophan, a Russian mystic from the nineteenth century, says that 'attention to what goes on in the heart and to what comes out of it is the chief work of a well-ordered Christian life . . . the outward and inward are brought into due relation with one another'. But he adds that attention is not enough, for we need discernment too, to sift our desires and motivations if we are to journey, rather than merely register. That journey, says Theophan, might initially be one of descent rather than ascent: 'One must descend with the mind into the heart, and there stand before the face of the Lord, ever present, all-seeing within you.' But this descent does eventually lead to ascent. For at these moments, there is liberty. Once the thoughts of the heart are cleansed, the purity and light lead to a new kind of illumination. The Kingdom is within you.

I am well aware that this may seem like a very strange way to open up the beginning of an academic year. But then again, light, stillness, attention, focus, to say nothing of paying attention to the state of the heart, is probably the only place to truly begin with us. So, what next? Let me say a couple of things briefly. A word that we often use in this college – and it is a term that has a great deal of currency in theological education – is 'formation'. It is easy enough to issue instructions to the apostles of the present and future, but how are the leaders of God's people to be formed? Yet you'd be right to be suspicious of a word like 'formation', and there are three types of legitimate objection to the term.

First, the metaphorical implication is that people are inert material, like clay lumps – passive, malleable and easily moulded – and therefore subject to the greater force doing the moulding. Second, those doing the forming are those in power – whereas we might want to say that all those in the learning community, and perhaps especially staff, are in a process of formation. Third, there is an implicit hint that there is a recipe or formula to correspond to – that there is a 'form' to become – and therefore one needs to be 'conformed'.

But true formation is not about a slavish correspondence to the past. To be sure, knowing, relating to and respecting the past is indeed vital – the Holy Spirit was alive and well in the history of our ancestors too. But the same Spirit that forms us now also calls us not just to formation, but to transformation. In that respect, the gospel commissions us to be sent out.

However, it does not give us a complete list of what you need for the end of the journey. It is, rather, a set of instructions for setting off. That is the point; we are not given everything we need to complete – merely what is required to make a start. Christ's call to 'follow me' is a start, not the final result.

And so, I begin by inviting you to get lost. I don't mean this rudely, of course. I mean by getting lost, that you may need the courage, and indeed some reassurance, that a degree of disorientation is both inevitable and desirable in training and formation. In order to seek God, you may need to get lost: just a little. Sometimes you may need to put away the familiar maps and compass, and allow yourself to find God in new places, people, experiences and ideas. Getting lost is all about finding the Lord of the Journey. Getting lost is about finding yourself in new ways. As Esther de Waal says in her fine book, *Seeking God*:

> The very top of the ladder carries a promise of the serenity that comes with my discovery that God is in charge of my life and that as a result I am finally free. I am released from my bondage to my self-seeking, my ambitions, my self-sufficiency and all the rest of it. This is of course New Testament teaching, that in God's service [we] find perfect freedom. (1984, p. 27)

De Waal points out that it is when we are a bit more broken, or perhaps a little lost, the possibility of journeying from slavery to freedom exists. It is ironic, I suppose, that at the very point of submission to God's gentle rule for our lives, we find true freedom. At the point of surrender, we find ourselves captive to something more wonderful than what we thought we wanted or desired. She continues:

> The only hope . . . is to throw myself on the support of God, relying on the protecting nearness of the God of the psalms who reaches out to me just as I felt that I could go no further. For obedience is a risky business. It is much easier to talk about it than to act it out. It means being prepared to take my life in my hands and place it in the hands of God. (de Waal, 1984, p. 28)

My hunch is that we are all here because God has called us. Not primarily to acquire more knowledge, competence and skills – though these are important. Or to acquire more novel tastes for ecclesiastical bling or esoteric rites and ceremonies – though these can be useful. No, we are beckoned: 'Follow me'. Because what the world needs from us, through Christ, is more holiness, more love, and clergy who embody this richly, truly and faithfully.

We'll do our level best here to help you follow him who has called you. But this is not a community of perfection. It has its rough edges. Things go wrong from time to time. Will you get everything right? Probably not. Will we as a staff get some things wrong. Yes. But being here is not about this; it is about following the one who calls us, and living together in love and charity, faith and hope. So, give yourself time. Give others time. Be good to yourself. Remember, we are all unfinished projects. The advice given by St Bernard of Clairvaux to young abbots seems to me to be particularly appropriate: 'Notice everything. Turn a blind eye to some things. Correct a little. Above all, cherish your brothers and sisters.'

Ultimately, the gospel challenges to us get going and follow; but also to relinquish our grip. The Church is not 'ours'; nor is its future shape. Let go; offer yourself; and let God shape. Surrender. The good thing about letting go is that God is likely to surprise you. The call of Matthew reminds us that if we abandon ourselves to God, we will not lose, but rather gain. It is a strange logic; indeed, a strange wisdom, which most with veiled eyes will never see. It is not the wisdom of the age, but something born of a higher wisdom that comes from God. 'Follow me' is not a plan; it is just a simple command to make a start.

Yet the logic of handing ourselves into the hands of God is something that our great mystical writers knew all about; before you can start, you have to stop, and realize that you have in one sense already arrived. Everything, said Bernard of Clairvaux – all the theological problems and issues you will ever encounter – needs to be 'cast in the perspective of God's never-ending and all-encompassing love'. Seeing that is what allowed Matthew to leave his tax booth and just walk off with Jesus. And Jesus says to you and I today, wherever we are, and whatever our hopes and fears, or reservations and expectations, 'Come, follow me.'

Article Thirty-Five: On Evelyn Underhill

Food for the journey

Readings: Wisdom 7.7–10, 15–16; I Corinthians 1.18–25; Matthew 4.1–9.

Here is some wisdom – from Schulz, the creator of Charlie Brown. In one of the more memorable cartoon strips, Lucy, hands on hips, addresses Charlie Brown and says there are only two types of people in this life. Those who sit on a deckchair at the back of the ship, gazing on what they are leaving behind and where they have come from, and those who sit at the front of the ship on a deckchair, looking to the future. 'Which kind of person are you, Charlie Brown?', she asks. Charlie Brown pauses, and then says, 'Neither – I really can't figure out how to get these deckchairs up.'

Wisdom is, by nature, surprising. In Daniel Hardy and David Ford's seminal *Jubilate: Theology in Praise*, the authors ask a teasing question quite early on. What, they ask, is the biggest or most fundamental problem facing the Church? There may be many nominations for answering this question. But Hardy and Ford, daringly, suggest that the biggest problem facing the Church is, apparently, 'coping with the overwhelming abundance of God . . .'. I'll repeat that: 'coping with the overwhelming abundance of God . . .'.

I think this must be true, and it is arguably truer – if things can be more true in one place than in another – in the Anglican Church, where we practise understatement with a skill and a passion that reflects our innate English identity. For in our mellow, mild and mature polity, we don't do abundance well. We like our religion to be interesting and rich – but also sedate: ordered, not overly fussy, and certainly not exuberant. So the idea that we are struggling to cope with God's overwhelming abundance might come as a surprise, and possibly a shock.

This is, of course, just what Hardy and Ford want to confront us with. For at the heart of the gospel is a God who can give more than we can ask or desire. Who gives without counting the cost. And who gives in almost immeasurable portions: our cup runneth over; the nets burst; we receive a hundredfold; he comes that we should have life, and life abundant; the manna falls; the spring rises; the desert blooms; the grain comes up – thirty, sixty, one hundredfold. The Gospels, like the rest of scripture, testify to a God who blesses richly and abundantly – more, as I say, than we can ask or desire. More.

Indeed, the only miracle to feature in the same way in all four Gospels seems to go out of its way to stress God's abundance. The feeding of the five thousand stresses the plentiful nature of God's provision. But each account by the four Evangelists leaves the teasing footnote, namely that there are baskets of leftovers as a result of this miracle. So much is provided and multiplied that there is an element of waste; food that might now have to be discarded. Or perhaps stored and hoarded; but leftovers nonetheless. More is given than is needed. God, it seems, is excessive, abundant and exuberant – and we mostly can't cope with his odd style of catering. You'd expect him to be more economic. But he isn't. He gives – and with exuberance. Helder Camara's poem (1974) catches this:

> Isn't your creation wasteful?
> Fruits never equal
> The seedlings' abundance.
> Springs scatter water.
> The sun gives out
> enormous light.
> May your bounty teach me
> greatness of heart.
> May your magnificence
> stop me being mean.
> Seeing you a prodigal
> and open-handed giver,

let me give unstintingly,
like a king's son.
like God's own.

The mention of 'prodigal' in the poem is interesting. Christian readers would naturally associate this word with the wayward son from Luke's Gospel (15.11–32). The word means 'wasteful' and 'reckless', as well as 'extravagant' and 'profligate'. But here, Camara uses the word of the father in the parable, and so of God himself. What is being suggested here? That our problematic prodigal-like tendencies are met by God's much stronger redemptive prodigal-like character. That he meets our deficiencies with his abundance.

So the poem conveys the interesting idea that God will use all manner of means and circumstances to demonstrate his goodness, abundance and extravagant, seemingly wasteful love. Even the manifest failures of the prodigal son (and indeed his elder brother) become opportunities for the father to demonstrate the overwhelming abundance of his love and devotion. So God, I think, does good things with our failures – if we are supple enough to yield rather than grasp. He will create redemptive and fulsome possibilities out of the places, spaces and times where we only see waste and loss. It is the case, as St Paul says, that 'all things work together for the good for those who love him'. All things. Even the failures. This is surely what Paul is driving at in our reading from I Corinthians: the base, foolish and seeming failures of the world turn out to be part of the wisdom of God.

It reminds me of another famous Peanuts cartoon by Schulz, in which Lucy is explaining to Charlie Brown that God uses our failures and disappointments for higher purposes. Charlie Brown seems very unsure about this, and starts thumbing through his personal history to check on Lucy's theology, before finally wailing 'but in my case he's got too much material to work with'. But God can indeed use it all.

This is one of the great lessons of the Old Testament. There is deliverance, salvation, success, a moral code to live by, a kingdom established – but then also exile. And God is in all of these. And it is tempting, sometimes, to see the exile as the failure, and representing the absence of God. 'By the waters of Babylon, we sat down and wept, remembering Zion . . . how shall we sing the Lord's song in a strange land?' Yet the exile is also part of God's abundant purpose; just a more difficult lesson. Wisdom is seeing that God does amazing things in the times we regard as wasted. He works in the wilderness and the darkness – because it is neither a wilderness nor darkness to God.

The Church, of course, will do its utmost to get out of exile and back to the promised land, and as soon as possible. In so doing, it sometimes forgets that God has laid this proscribed period upon us in order to allow us to reflect; or perhaps to become leaner; or maybe even to chasten us. In Babylon, you can hear the Anglican voices of compromise, innovation and modernization whispering in the ears of the priests. 'Of course, I'm not saying abandon Jehovah . . . it's just that the Babylonians are doing very well, and we could give their gods a bit of a try – see how they work for a bit . . . no harm done.'

One presumes that the Israelites struggled with the same indices of success in relation to their faith that the Church wrestles with. Losing numbers, falling congregations? Why not try a spiffy postmodern course that draws people into church? Don't hit them with doctrine; woo them with pasta, chardonnay and fellowship. Or, just update your message and ditch all the complex and irrelevant jargon. Say less about judgement and confession: stress love. You'll pack 'em in.

The Old Testament prophets, though, will have none of it. Their message to us, in the face of apparent failure and interminable exile, is simple and uncompromising. In many ways, that message can be summed up in one word, and indeed it also sums up the Old Testament: wait. Yes, wait. Wait for God's good time. Learn the lesson from apparent failure. Try and see history and destiny through his eyes, not ours. This, of course, requires a special patience. To wait – sometimes in darkness – for his timing and light is no easy task. For it sometimes means being with a community or individuals that are apparently diminished, yet being the leader that holds out the vision for replenishment and plenty.

Here, we are to be the ministers who remind God's people that there are losses and gains, but that in God's economy, and given patience, even the losses will be transfigured. We have to wait for God's goodness and completeness to gestate, for he surely feeds us even when we struggle to see the manna in his hand.

Speaking of hunger, a final word. One of my predecessors at Cuddesdon set up a 'God on Monday' Club some years ago. The Club was open to all, and there was only one rule. You could only talk about God. Not about the Church. Or about ecclesiastical tat and fashions. Or about Mass. Or about the next Archbishop of Canterbury. Or about the latest gossip on preferment. Only about God – nothing more, nothing less. It is surprising to discover just how tricky this can be.

But Evelyn Underhill, whom we commemorate here, knew all about this. Writing to Archbishop Cosmo Gordon Lang, on the eve of the 1930 Lambeth Conference, she had the temerity to remind him that the world was not especially hungry for what was about to happen at the forthcoming conference. Funnily enough, she said, and despite media absorption, the world is not very interested in our politics, preferment or proclivities. Tat and tactics may get us excited from time to time, but Underhill put the main agenda pretty sharply in her letter: 'May it please your Grace . . . I desire to humbly suggest that the interesting thing about religion is . . . God . . . and the people are hungry for God.'

That is wisdom. So all I want to say is this: there is nothing you can do that will make God love you any less or any more. God's love for you is complete, abundant and overwhelming.

Article Thirty-Six: On Thomas Ken, Nonjuror

Beyond Labels

Readings: Philippians 4.4–9 and Luke 6.17–23.

I think there are two types of people in this life. Those who read labels, instructions and recipes before opening packets, boxes and proceeding to start assembling, cooking or whatever – and those who don't. For those in the middle, like me, it is not so much an antipathy for reading these things as it is failing to make any sense of them. IKEA is the worst. 'IKEA', as you know, is a subtle Swedish mnemonic for 'invite your neighbour round, who has a toolkit, and who may actually know what they are doing'. I do not. The phrase 'flat-packed for your convenience' is, to me, a cruel taunt.

Labels on packaging are no better. Have you noticed how pointless some of them are in our risk-averse society? On a bag of pistachios – 'may contain nuts': note the 'may'. A carton of juice might state, 'Warning: potential choking hazard' – but only if you thought you might have a stab at swallowing the thing whole. Or, on a carton of milk, 'To consume, open at other end' is another favourite. And in nearly every case, long notices are concluded, rather mockingly in my view, with these words: 'Always read the label.' You couldn't read it unless you had.

As with most things, long before consumerism got into the business of labelling and packaging, religion was there before it. Not always with great results, either. It is perhaps okay to think that on a given day we shall celebrate 'St Barnabas the Encourager' – a nice epithet for any of us. But consider poor old 'James the Lesser'. I am not sure about you, but this strikes me as being a little less complimentary. 'Lesser' in what aspects, exactly? You can almost hear the sniggering at the back of class at this one. And which of us would like to be known for being minor rather than major keys? Labelling might be accurate, but it can also be constricting and constraining: 'Mark the shorter'; 'Martyn the younger', 'Raymond the elder', for example; or even 'Margaret the Northerner'. See what sort of fun you could have with the people around you.

So what, then, are we to make of 'Thomas Ken, Nonjuror'? And why, exactly, does it make any sense at all to preach on him at this, our Leavers' Service? One brief and obvious answer is simply to state that none of us should be judged by, or buy into, the reductionism that accompanies a label. Those of you about to be ordained will be inducted into the world of ecclesial and pastoral shorthand: brief, summary 'labels' that try to encapsulate persons and situations. It is, of course, a way of learning quickly – but the simplicity can be deceptive. It is easy to collude with the headlines that say 'he's trouble', 'she's difficult', 'he's fragile', 'she's unreliable', 'they're awkward', or 'that family isn't what it seems'. To say nothing of 'catholic', 'evangelical', 'liberal' or 'happy clappy'.

But I guess, if we have taught you anything here, by simply living in community, it is not to be deceived by superficial labels. There is more to a person or persons than meets the eye. It takes time to discover people's gifts and potential – and most especially in otherness, strangeness and the unfamiliar. Sure, always read the label – but don't confuse the description with the goods that are actually on offer.

Thomas Ken might be rather weary of being known and listed as 'Nonjuror'. Born in Berkhamsted, he was ordained in 1662, the year of Charles II's Restoration. After serving in a very poor parish in Winchester diocese, and being Chaplain at Winchester College, he was consecrated as Bishop of Bath and Wells. So far, so good. But trouble came with the accession of the Roman Catholic James II to the throne. James II proposed to rescind the Restoration penal laws, and Thomas, and six fellow bishops, felt in conscience that they could not comply. They were imprisoned for this on 8 June 1688.

But good news – or so it may have seemed – was not far off. In the Orange Revolution, James II fled, and the relatively bloodless coup saw William and Mary take the throne. Thomas was released from prison, and free to return to his episcopal duties. Except that he felt a vow was a vow, and an oath was an oath – and that he could not forswear his allegiance to James II, who was still his living and anointed monarch. Unable to make a new oath to a new king, Thomas was deprived of his see, and retired, spending his final years writing hymns, many of which are still sung to this day.

What do we take from this, you may wonder? Obviously, one lesson is that conscience matters – sometimes even more than preferment. Expressed more seriously, we might say that there is a cost in discipleship, and sometimes that cost is considerable in terms of sacrifice.

Whether or not you agree with Thomas Ken's choice is beside the point. What cannot be denied, however, is that he chose the gospel over his continuance and furtherance in the Church. And yet, with what one can only assume was monumental charity and grace on his part, he continued to contribute to the same Church that had wounded and deprived him. There is love; costly love that gives, and does not count the cost. This is why I rather dislike the 'Nonjuror' label. Thomas Ken shouldn't be defined by what he wasn't, but by what he was – a writer of hymns, a pastor and a man of integrity who put his discipleship and spirituality above his (lost) preferment. Faithfulness mattered more than 'success'. I don't expect for a moment that many of us will have to make the kind of dramatic choice that Thomas Ken had to make. But what can we take from his life and example to help us in our formation? Several things merit mention.

First, don't be afraid of weakness. Thomas Ken knows well that he holds treasure in clay jars – and he is the clay. It is this that allows him to move aside, and into a kind of self-imposed retirement. For he knows this is not the end. No matter how the rancorous politics that threaten to overwhelm him are resolved, Thomas Ken knows that he is afflicted but not crushed, persecuted but not forsaken, struck down but not destroyed.

Second, there is a patience in his work and example that exhibits a genuine wisdom. Here is someone committed to the long game, who has understood that the Christian life is lived more in waiting and hope than in results. He is alert, and does not cede to despair. Even in his post-episcopal phase, he turns his mind to creativity when it could have easily capitulated to bitterness. All of us encounter projects and persons in ministry that either fail to turn out to be all that we hoped, or can even become arenas of defeat.

Third, Thomas Ken is priestly and principled. There is something prayerfully methodical about this man. Underpinning his commitments we do not find stubbornness or pig-headedness, but rather integrity and resolve that lead him to take a path that loosens his relationship with power and privilege. I like this – it is a good pattern to contemplate as we are formed and re-formed for ministry. He understands his vocation as a release, not something that is to be grasped. St John of the Cross knew this all too well:

> To reach satisfaction in all,
>   desire its possession in nothing.
> To come to possess all,
>   desire the possession of nothing.
> To arrive at being all,
>   desire to be nothing.
> To come to the knowledge of all,
>   desire the knowledge of nothing.

(*The Ascent of Mount Carmel*, Book 1, chapter 13.11, 2008, p. 109)

So, I am not especially keen on this 'Thomas Ken, Nonjuror' label in the lectionary. There is more to him than that. And I suppose that is my point. Just as there is much more to each and every one of you that is preparing for ordination than the epithets and nicknames that you'll get. To be sure, you'll be labelled, and sometimes the temptation to label all you encounter is irresistible. We all know, of course, that labelling and categorization is needed to begin with, so we can make sense of things and order and process what we see and what is happening to us. But look deeper. Look beyond superficial descriptions and the easy labels that abound in the Church. As one recent writer puts it:

> Martin Luther's central theological insight was that only when you have given up trying to make it under your own steam can you adopt a proper attitude of reliance upon God. Failure is the beginning of success. It's a high-risk strategy emotionally. A bit like that game where you fall backwards trusting that someone will catch you. (Fraser, 2012, p. 24)

That is when we can begin to discover the riches of God's light and treasure in the earthenware. We discover the saint in the nonconformist, the spiritual person in the apparently awkward pedantic rebel, or the person of deep principle and integrity who just seemed, superficially, to have become obsessed with rules.

In other words, look for the Christ in the odd, the alien, the stranger, the awkward and the unexpected. Find him in the desert places and in apparent failure, not just in apparent success. And in your diaconal and priestly formation, remember that he often comes to us in the unfamiliar. And even when the chips are down, stick at it with prayer, hope and love. Because Christ will use your faithfulness, which will always matter far more than success. As Paul reminds us, God has said, 'let light shine out darkness' – and it is this God who has shone in our hearts, to give the light of the knowledge of the glory of God in face of Jesus Christ. It is the case, I suppose, that nothing less than his face is what we seek to be reflected in our own expression: his compassion, empathy, joy, peace and tenderness.

So, if we can embody something of this in our lives and ministries, we will, God willing, be difficult to label. But we will be wonderful to know – not for what we have done or not done, but for what we are; for being not doing. For people will say, perhaps of you and me, that they have maybe caught a glimpse of God. It is to this that we are called; to hold the treasure in jars of clay, as Paul says, 'so that it may be made clear that this extraordinary power belongs to God and does not come from us'.

Be open, then, to what is coming. See beyond the labels. Be yourselves – the wonderful self that God has already made you, and is moulding – the pot that God has shaped and is shaping. It may go well; it may go pear-shaped, sometimes. No matter. Whatever happens, be faithful. Remember that you have been and are loved by all of us here, and also prayed for just as you are. We rejoice in the work that God is doing in you, and will do through you. Pray for us, too, as we will continue to pray for you. And may God give you grace and courage to follow all his saints in faith, in hope and love, wherever that may be.

Article Thirty-Seven: On St Alban

Learning and living in God

Readings: John 12.24–26 and 2 Timothy 2.1–4

Towards the end of the classic Pixar movie *Toy Story* (1995), Woody and Buzz Lightyear find themselves in great peril as they attempt to catch up with Andy's mother's car . . . the big removal has happened. The packers have come, and everyone is leaving home to start a new life in a new place. Except that both Buzz and Woody are left behind and, needing to catch up fast, Buzz is forced to fly, except that it is not exactly flying – more of a big catapult, really. As Woody says, 'That's not flying – that's just falling with style.' It reminds me of Douglas Adams in *Life, the Universe, and Everything*: 'There is an art to flying. The knack lies in learning how to throw yourself at the ground – and miss' (Adams, 1982, p. 1).

'That's not flying – that's just falling with style' might just serve as our text for this evening. When we speak of falling, we can barely conceive of it in positive terms. To fall is dangerous: I have had a fall, and broken a bone. Speaking of fallen leaders and fallen men or women implies some sort of disgrace. The Fall is the end of the creation story in Genesis, and the beginning of an epic salvation story. Jesus falls on the *Via Dolorosa*. So why does he seem to suggest that we need to fall? 'Unless a grain of wheat falls to the ground and dies . . .'. Jesus did not say 'unless a grain of wheat is planted'. He said 'fall'. To fall is to fail; our downfall is our worst moment, is it not? Cities fall – so do people. It is to be reduced: to come to nothing. And yet, we also fall in love. To fall is also to let go. It is also to go with the flow; to cascade, like a river or waterfall. What, then, can Jesus mean by asking us to fall, and not fly – to fall with style? Here is a poem by Rainer Maria Rilke, from his *Book of Hours: Love Poems to God*:

How surely gravity's law,
strong as an ocean current,
takes hold of even the strongest thing
and pulls it toward the heart of the world.

Each thing –
each stone, blossom, child –
is held in place.
Only we, in our arrogance,
push out beyond what we belong to
for some empty freedom.

If we surrendered
to earth's intelligence
we could rise up rooted, like trees.

Instead we entangle ourselves
in knots of our own making
and struggle, lonely and confused.

So, like children, we begin again
to learn from the things,
because they are in God's heart;
they have never left him.

This is what the things can teach us:
to fall,
patiently to trust our heaviness.
Even a bird has to do that
before he can fly.

As Woody says, less of the flying – and more of the falling with
style. Ministry is very much about falling in to God, and less about
struggling than we may think. Even with flesh and blood, and the
Church, and the PCC . . .

So, here we are, ready to bid farewell and pray for those about
to be ordained. And our readings for the day serve up those for
St Alban. We have the exhortation from 2 Timothy 2.1–4 to be a

good soldier of Christ. And from the Gospel of John, an apparently opaque agrarian reference to a grain of wheat falling, dying and rising. And all set within the context of Chapter 12. First, Jesus is anointed; then the triumphal entry into Jerusalem happens, with Jesus being proclaimed Messiah and leader. Then some Greeks seek him out: 'Sir, we want to see Jesus', before Jesus speaks about his death – the first time he does so in John's Gospel.

But what of Alban? According to Bede's *Ecclesiastical History of the English People*, Alban was a pagan living in the Roman settlement of Verulamium (now St Albans), who converted to Christianity, and was executed by decapitation on a hill above the town. Alban sheltered a Christian priest in his home, and was converted and baptized by him. When the Roman soldiers went to Alban's house to look for the priest, Alban exchanged cloaks with him, and was arrested in his stead at Chantry Island.

Alban was taken before the magistrate, who was furious at the deception and ordered that Alban be given the punishment due to the priest if he had indeed become a Christian. Alban declared, 'I worship and adore the true and living God who created all things.' These words are still used in a prayer at St Albans Abbey. St Alban was eventually sacrificed to the Roman gods and was condemned to death. He was taken out of the town across the River Ver to the top of the hill opposite. The reputed place of his beheading is where St Albans Cathedral now stands.

So when Jesus says, 'I am the vine, and you are the branches', he is speaking about some very real connections. He is saying, I suppose, that the you and I, the Church, are very real extensions of his body. By tasting the fruit of the vine from the branches, you will know something of the real quality of the true vine; we are connected, and we live in a world of deep and intricate connections. Thus, unless a grain of wheat falls to the ground and dies, it cannot bear fruit. For there to be flourishing, there must be sacrifice: no pain, no gain. I imagine in some small way that Jesus' words in the Gospel of John give us a new perspective on such connections. And significantly, the fourth Evangelist places these words in a context in which the road is wide open.

I speak, of course, about Jesus' triumphal entry into Jerusalem in the first part of John 12, where the prophecies of Isaiah all seem to be coming true. The way is prepared; the crowds cry 'hosanna'; the Lord has come. But just at the very epoch of this epiphany, the Evangelist attributes these words to Jesus – a kind of reflection on what is actually happening, under the surface of the crowd's adulation: 'unless a grain of wheat falls into the ground and dies, it remains a single grain. But if it dies, it bears much fruit.'

The connection here is one of paradox. Unless we step aside – die to ourselves – we cannot bear fruit. We must yield ourselves, our power, our identity, our heritage, ourselves – so that what God longs to give birth to will grow and flourish. This is no easy lesson, to be sure.

Dennis Potter, the playwright, had something wise to say before he died: 'Religion is not the bandage – it is the wound.' Yes, we turn to Christ and the Church for comfort, hope and healing. But in receiving it, we are marked by the cross, which requires us to expend our own lives sacrificially in offering and gift. We are asked not to fly, but first to fall – into his arms, and into a kind of death.

And then there are the searching Greeks. Presumably they made up part of the crowd on that first Palm Sunday. They are not Jewish, so are just a bit confused by all the commotion. But they are intrigued too, and so seek out a disciple – Philip in this case – and ask one of the great questions of the New Testament, indeed of all time: 'Sir, we want to see Jesus.' Sir, we want to see Jesus. The Gospel does not tell us that their wish was granted. But I think we can assume it was. For Jesus responds with a speech that starts with grain and ends with him predicting his death. If you want to see Jesus, you'll have to look not at a throne, but at the cross. Not a place of power, but a place of pain and torment.

As the Gospels regularly hint, it is the example that makes the difference, not the ideas; the praxis, not the theories. The call to discipleship remains compellingly simple: to be like him; to love one another as he loves us; to bear fruit that will last; and to love those who have no one to love them. As Jesus says: 'unless a grain of wheat falls into the earth and dies, it remains a single grain . . . but if it dies, it bears much fruit . . .'

In our Church today there is much talk of leadership. Far too much talk of strategy and vision, and way too much attention to organization, as though this were somehow the most important thing. The life of Alban and the words of Jesus suggest something rather different to me. The gentleness and hospitality of Alban led directly to his death. He protected, fed and kept the priest who sought refuge in his house. He lived his life in Christ, and, in so doing, exposed himself. Alban gave to that priest what Christ asks of us today: will you love your people through cherishing and protecting, and enabling their nourishing and flourishing?

And that is our question. Can you love and serve others – putting all before your self – and yet not count the cost? Can you, at the same time, radiate warmth, peace, openness and hospitality. To be a beam of God's light and warmth in a world that is sometimes dark and cold? Can your friends and colleagues say, hand on heart, that to know you is to somehow have been touched by the presence of God?

So on this day for Alban, and for those preparing for ordained ministry, we begin to see some other connections. We begin to realize that when Jesus speaks about being 'lifted up from the earth' in order to 'draw all people' to himself and God, he is probably not talking about a heavenly throne – well at least not yet. He is, rather, speaking of the cross. Here he hangs, tortured and dying on the tree. Indeed, he is lifted up. Sir, we want to see Jesus. Yes, behold your king, hanging there for you.

This army that God has called us to is like no other. And the races he asks us to run are mostly marathons, not sprints – and with few laurels at the end. Points don't mean prizes, alas. But do not worry. Let us serve the one who led not by dominating, but by serving. The one who led not by triumphing, but by sacrificing. The one who led not by being first on the podium, but by falling to the ground, and dying. It is from here we rise – for all resurrections, and all ordinations, require us to give ourselves fully to God; to fall to and for him; to die with him, so that we might not only be raised, but also see the fruit grow from the many seeds that God is, even now, seeking to sow in his world.

So, don't worry too much about flying. Fall with style. As Buzz might say, to infinity, and beyond.

Article Thirty-Eight: On Edward King, Bishop of Lincoln

The ministry of hospitality

Readings: Ezekiel 34.11–16; Hebrews 13.1–8; Matthew 5.10–12

'Let mutual love continue. Do not neglect to show hospitality to strangers, for by doing that some have entertained angels without knowing it (Heb. 13.1–2).'

Like many clergy, I have spent a good deal of time sitting with folk who are preparing to die. It is, unfailingly, a moving experience: both profound and a privilege. I particularly recall spending time, as a curate in Bedford (a county town that was once part of Lincoln diocese), sitting with a frail elderly woman in one of the many nursing and residential homes we looked after in our parish, as she moved gently from this life into the next, only occasionally recovering consciousness to talk about her hopes and fears, and about her faith.

One day, she told me a story of how she had met an angel. The year was 1970 – and Enoch Powell had made his famous 'rivers of blood' speech just 18 months earlier. Bedford was fertile territory for Powell's cultural concerns – a place that had welcomed many immigrants from Asia, Africa, the Caribbean and the Far East in the post-war era – yet was also a rather conservative county town. Tensions were very apparent, and trouble was brewing.

My friend – the woman who was slipping into the next life as I held and stroked her frail hand – told me of how she had gone down to the town hall one evening in winter, to attend a meeting for residents who were concerned about the growing numbers of immigrants. It had been an uneasy few hours, with impassioned speeches and much angst. And when it ended, she stepped outside, only to discover the town covered in a thick blanket of fog – a real pea-souper, courtesy of the River Ouse. But she made her way to her little Morris Minor, and as she was unlocking the car door, a large man appeared from behind, and gripped her tightly to himself.

She did not know how, but she had caught just enough of a glimpse of him to know that he was black, weighed about 15 stone, and was about six foot two. But he held her from behind, and so tightly that she could hardly breathe. She could not scream either. Yet she found herself feeling unusually composed, and then, for what seemed like an age, but can only have been a few seconds, she realized the man was weeping. She struggled for breath, and then found herself asking him what was wrong.

He replied, through sobs, that he was hopelessly lost. He had just arrived from Caricou – a small island in the south of the Caribbean – and had never seen fog or mist like this. He was afraid. His grip relaxed and, slightly to her amazement, she found herself driving him across town, where she dropped him off. When they got to the address, he turned to her and said that he had prayed to God that night – that he would send an angel to guide him to his family, living on the other side of town, miles from the railway station. And that God had answered his prayer. After he had left, the woman broke down in tears, and went home.

As she told me the story, I asked her why she had remembered this, and especially now? Because, she said, he had prayed for an angel to guide him. But in actual fact, she was no angel. Rather, he was the angel God had sent to her: he was the stranger in disguise. The man made her confront her fears; she realized that the strangers she was being taught to fear needed help and welcome; that she could entertain an angel.

Edward King would have warmed to such a story. As a curate in Wheatley, then as Chaplain and later Principal of Cuddesdon, he had a reputation for being a messenger of peace and consolation, of not only visiting the sick, but of finding Christ in these encounters. Later still, as a beloved Bishop of Lincoln diocese, he sat and prayed with condemned criminals, and stood by them as they dropped through the hangman's door, straight into God's arms.

For King, the Christian life was one of discovery, brightness and wisdom – not doctrinaire or formulaic. Although he exercised

considerable personal spiritual discipline, he was often remembered, in his early ministry, for his light touch – 'gaiety' was the
word used a century ago – and for his warmth and holiness. As
a college principal, from 1863 to 1873, his students remarked on
the model of Anglican life he cultivated at Cuddesdon: 'a relaxed
though disciplined community life – a minimum of rules without
stiff formality – a true fellowship of staff and students'.

Perhaps even more remarkably, and for a Victorian too, King
saw that the Christian life was one where ordinands best discovered and developed their vocations in what he termed the 'Christian
higgledy-piggledy': in humanity, as well as divinity; in ordinary life,
as well as lavish liturgy. For King, Christian wisdom lay in learning
to balance passion with objectivity. He said in one of his spiritual
letters, 'we must let our faith and doctrine be continually smashed
up', allow our schemes and plans to be broken. God comes in
through the mess and miscibility of life. We don't lose God in the
muddle; it is in the mix that we find him. Theology, for King, was
something not so much that you thought about and wrote about; it
was something you did with your life. He was one of the first expo-
nents of English pastoral theology in modern times.

So under King, Cuddesdon College shed its rigorist tendencies,
becoming a community that was pastoral, broad and explorative –
all of which he took to his professorship of pastoral theology, and
later to the see of Lincoln, from where, one century on, he is still
remembered and celebrated with much love and great affection.

On becoming Bishop of Lincoln, he is said to have remarked, 'I am
glad it is John Wesley's diocese – I shall be the Bishop of the Poor.'
He moved from the palace at Riseholme to the smaller medieval palace next to the cathedral, and thereby made himself accessible to his
clergy and to the people of the city. At his consecration, he remarked
that he looked forward to becoming a 'big curate' in the diocese.
He set aside many of the conventions and customs that his fellow
bishops took for granted. King wore old boots, lived simply, and
was often seen about in pretty worn-out clothes. If a confirmand
missed confirmation through illness, he would go to the house – any
house – and confirm at the bedside. The fact that King's picture can
still be found in many vestries up and down the diocese is a testimony
to what he mainly was as a bishop: a shepherd.

And speaking of shepherds, then, what kinds of lessons do our readings, and King's life and legacy, leave with us today? I guess that the trouble with us Christians is that we have taken far too many of the stories, parables and analogies about sheep and shepherding in scripture and used them as images of comfort and security for own ends. The result is that the texts – which undoubtedly are there to comfort those who are unsure, insecure and hoping in the midst of doubt – have been mostly used to exclude people, and not include them. But we forget that Jesus left 99 sheep to go and find just one. True, he is the true shepherd of the true flock; but also the shepherd who lays down his life for the sheep – and perhaps particularly for the ones that are lost.

When we look at the customary use of familiar texts in the Gospels – such as 'I am the way, the truth and the life', 'I am the good shepherd, and my sheep know my voice', 'no one comes to the Father but by me' and 'in my Father's house there are many rooms' – we remember how these words have been used to sift and exclude the alien, the stranger, and those with doubts, fears and uncertainties. But it is to these folk that God extends his hand, opens his heart, and ushers them into his mansion. It is to the lost sheep – the 'sheep not of this fold' – for whom he is also the shepherd. As Ezekiel says, and later echoed in the Gospels, 'I will seek the lost, and I will bring back the strayed.'

So at a time when precision in faith and practice in our worldwide Anglican Communion is sometimes seen to be so necessary, it is good to recall King's own fondness for 'Christian higgledy-piggledy', and remember that God's heaven has rather fuzzy edges. God, indeed, seems intent on welcoming the many, and not just a certain few. Even the ones who only stretch out their feeble hands to touch his cloak find healing in Jesus. It is enough. There is a wideness in God's mercy, as the hymn says, a wideness like the sea; but we make his love too narrow, with a strictness and zeal he will not own. God's welcome is more open and loving than ours; there is liberty and charity in his Kingdom.

Our churches, at their best, are communities of being, love, thought and worship, rather than being definitive bodies that have arrived at solid confessional closure. So we remain open, even if we risk being indecisive. Because we want to exclude . . .

no one. And we want to include . . . everyone. As Ezekiel reminds us today, God is a shepherd who will search for his sheep. He will not abandon those whom the Church has sometimes given up on. He will not reject; he will embrace. And you and I are invited to join with Edward King to help make our churches into places that reflect the broad compass of heaven, to be a sign of that ultimate open-gated community – a profoundly inclusive sheepfold.

Bill Vanstone, the great twentieth-century Anglican spiritual writer, used to have a nice line about the Church of England. Why, he asked, is it like a swimming pool? Answer: all the noise comes from the shallow end. And that's the challenge, is it not? Not to try and make yourself heard above the noise of church life, but rather prayerfully to immerse ourselves in the depths of God's love. To ponder the legacy of Edward King today is to reflect on a profound spiritual mentor, much-loved bishop and towering college principal.

And he would have loved this Eucharist today. A religious community of Sisters that he did much to encourage, coming together with a college he did so much to shape, worshipping in one sacred space. But all this is also to see something else: that in the simplicity of his profound commitment to a gospel of inclusion – Christ's love for all, seen in the face of the stranger, poor, prisoner, beggar, tortured – we have an Anglican saint who had a depth of faith that invites us to share in this shepherding. Just as Christ entertains us with his hospitality, so he would have us and our ministries be those that reflect God's hospitality. As our Collect today has it, 'Fill us, we pray, with tender sympathy and joyful faith, that we may also win others to know the love that passes knowledge, through him who is the shepherd and guardian of our souls, Jesus Christ . . .'

Article Thirty-Nine: On George Herbert

Praying for the Church

Readings: Malachi 2.5–7 and Matthew 11.25–30.

The Church of England, on the whole, is a little uncomfortable with heroes. An understated ecclesiology coupled to a reserved English manner makes for a nation – or at least a national church – that is, well, just too polite, settled and civilized to get very enthusiastic about anything. As one commentator has recently noted, can it really be any accident that cricket is the preferred game of the clergy in the Church of England? An individual, yet collaborative game; full of manners, codes of conduct – 'sporting' sport; strenuous and restful by turns, combining subtlety and strength (speed is rarely valued); where all may have different gifts and functions, yet be equally valued; and where the side about to lose can gain an honourable or even heroic draw, either due to rain or bad light. Results really don't matter; it's how you play the game.

I could go on. The other game that clergy play a lot of is chess (with their own magazine, *Chess Minister*). It is all about plots, pace and plans; a surrogate for the PCC. So, please, don't get me on to the ecclesiological and psychological significance of clergy and model railway clubs – you can probably begin to work that out for yourselves; it's all to do with things running to order, and on time – quite unlike normal ministry.

George Herbert is sometimes described as a 'founder' of Anglicanism. We commemorate him on 27 February. A modest man, he would be puzzled by this gathering, and perhaps the fact that he is remembered at all. Born in 1593, he went to Cambridge in 1514, where he became Public Orator. He was then an MP before surprising everyone by turning to the priesthood, having spent some time with his friend Nicholas Ferrar at Little Gidding. He went to the parish of Bemerton in 1630 as Rector, and it is here that he wrote his hymns and books, *The Temple* and *The Country Parson*. He died in 1633.

So what of our readings, and today's contender for patron saint of Anglicanism? Especially since Anglicans seem to be unable to avoid making a drama out of a crisis. On issues of major gravity, all the noise comes from the shrill reactionary voices that grab the headlines. The voices from the deep are seldom heard – the real words we need to hear are drowned out by the splashing and the shouting. But listen to Herbert on prayer, and you get something very different in terms of depth:

Prayer the Churches banquet, Angels age,
   Gods breath in man returning to his birth,
   The soul in paraphrase, heart in pilgrimage,
The Christian plummet sounding heav'n and earth;
Engine against th'Almightie, sinner's towre,
   Reversed thunder, Christ-side-piercing spear,
   The six daies world-transposing in an houre,
A kinde of tune, which all things heare and fear;
Softnesses, and peace, and joy, and love, and blisse,
   Exalted Manna, gladnesse of the best
   Heaven in ordinarie, man well drest,
The milkie way, the bird of Paradise,
   Church-bells beyond the stars heard, the souls bloud,
   The land of spices, something understood. (Herbert, 2004, p.38)

Nothing complicated or fussy here; pure and simple words that carry God's love. So, theologically, Herbert is neither 'liberal' nor 'conservative', but rather 'orthodox'. It is all about simple things: God loves us, and that is the good news to share in our daily lives and ministry. This is the only truly profound knowledge any priest guards with their lips. God has revealed some simple things to us; he loves us, and asks that we love one another as he as loves us.

I don't think the story we have in the Gospel today is accidental: the healing of the man on the Sabbath. Jesus makes him well – an act of profound compassion. But he also takes on the social and religious forces of apathy and antipathy that have so fearfully neglected and rejected the man who needed healing. So Jesus does two things in our Gospel: he heals with love and compassion, and he also takes on the alienating forces that failed the man – a profoundly political act.

When I look at the Gospels, I see that Jesus mostly healed the marginalized and dispossessed, those without means or status, the excluded and the castigated, the despised and rejected. Liberation theology has taught me to see the world, and healing, differently. Not to judge about whether or not healing happens, but rather to be mindful of the places of poverty and neglect where the cause and effects of disease and illness are all too apparent. These are the places where Christ loves and loves to be at work, through you and me, and his Church, his body.

So, where does all this leave us? Well, back with George Herbert, a worldly wise, world-affirming sixteenth-century cleric, who wrote hymns, wrote about ministry and talked about widespread participation and interdependence in the Church through the Eucharist and our life together. It suggests three things to me.

First, Anglicans agree with Jesus, in the Gospel reading set for Herbert's day from Matthew, that 'the Father reveals truth to children and to infants, and hides it from the wise'. As a Church, we can often assume that the only people who understand it are intelligent folk. Herbert saw that the truth of the Church lay in its pastoral heart, not simply its doctrines or dogma. Second, how you argue within a church, or undertake disputes, is often as important as the result. Look how Jesus debates – with clarity, but also with civility. Third, the Church of Christ is a complex *space*, and one through which we move throughout our lives.

God's temple is, quite literally, encompassing – it is big enough for all, and invites us all in. So, Herbert knew what Jesus proclaimed and practised: in God's Kingdom, all are welcome. Our job is not that of the Pharisees. We are not asked to be the gatekeepers or border-control police, but recruiters and welcomers for his Kingdom. That is what we pray for God's Church: that we would welcome all as God welcomes all.

Part Five: For Good Measure

Article Forty: On a Commemoration

Models of ministry – celebrating 20 years of the Revd Prof. Mark Chapman's ministry at Cuddesdon

Readings: Deuteronomy 26.16–end and Matthew 5.41–end.

This is partly a sermon about Richard Hooker: more on him shortly. But to begin with, my text today might easily be from 2 Timothy 4.11: 'Get Mark and bring him with you, because he may be useful to me in my ministry.' Somehow, 'useful' doesn't quite do enough for me. So what can we say about the Gospel today, and perhaps about our illustrious colleague and friend, Mark? (Not the Mark of Paul's letter to Timothy, but this one – Mark Chapman, dean of the college and our beloved vice-principal.)

Mark is that rare thing in ministry: a true tonic. Precisely what you need in an institution like this, or a village like this, or in the Church and academy, or the vain, vaulted spheres of a General Synod. And the recipe for that same tonic provides some important clues as to why he is so often, unfailingly, in fact, useful. He is prepared to be subversive, and ask the awkward questions.

This is fused with the quiet and understated scholarliness of a man with the active and reflective mind of a radical, which, in turn, is fused with a pastoral heart that wants the best, seeks the best and thinks the best – of all. For some in ordained ministry, this simply means being nice to as many people as possible, and avoiding confrontation. But in Mark's case, there is a kick to this tonic – one that does not duck the difficult discussions and decisions that are needed if ministries and institutions are to flourish.

Everything I know about Mark leads to me to conclude that – in much the way that Rowan Williams once described Desmond Tutu – he knows how to enjoy himself. And from that there springs up a profound security that gives a solid foundation to a ministry rooted in love and acceptance. It has been there from the beginning. It is rooted in his upbringing – socialist and Anglo-Catholic – which brings us the beguiling blend of the faithful subversive, which is also securely grounded in his scholarship and spirituality. In being true to ourselves – how we are both created and redeemed – and in putting love and commitment first, we have the only true basis for any subsequent vocation. And that is Mark – friend, confidant, critic, comic – wickedly so, sometimes – but above all, given, and ours.

I don't know if you have ever seen anything of the old TV series *MASH*. Set in the Korean War, *MASH* – Mobile Army Surgical Hospital – follows the fortunes of doctors and nurses as they try and stitch up American troops and send them back home. Not necessarily whole, but at least alive. It is what the critics call 'dramedy' – a fusion of dark, ironic comedy with drama and moments of hilarity. Even if you have only seen the original film, you'll still have a sense of what dramedy is.

But the TV series – one of the most peerless pieces of scriptwriting in modern times – is something that does profound things to our minds and hearts as we watch and engage in the challenges faced by the doctors and nurses during a war. Based on the 1968 novel by Richard Hooker – the American writer, not the other one – we have some of the best dark comedy to have emerged in the post-war period.

Of course, we have our own version of MASH here. 'MASH' might stand for 'Modest Anglican Seminary on the Hill'. Year by year, folk arrive at Cuddesdon, and are worked upon by the genius of our qualified team, before being sent out again for ministry. But I must confess that I sometimes feel that in my role as principal here, I have been terribly miscast. I would like to think of myself as a kind of Hawkeye Pierce (played by Alan Alda in the TV series, and Donald Sutherland in the film). But I am in fact surprised to be Colonel Potter, leading with a mixture of benign tolerance and detached empathy.

If you know MASH at all, you'll know that we see the hospital *through* the wit and wisdom of Hawkeye Pierce. It is Hawkeye who combines affectionate scepticism with cynicism and compassion, who brings both laughter and insight, who is not afraid to be deeply critical and radical, yet also clearly loves the institution he serves in all is brokenness and goodness. Hawkeye is the lens through which we see war and suffering at its worst, but also the best of humanity, and ultimately hope. It is in his pathos, empathy, concern, pithy wisdom, sharp wit – but above all, his humanity – that we see the possibilities of healing and redemption. If you can find light and laughter in this war, Hooker says, then humanity has some hope. Hawkeye is not only our guide for this, he is also somehow the embodiment of such possibilities.

I think the parallels are striking, and they hardly need sketching here. To be sure, seminaries are not hospitals. But they can be places of intense work and labour, as well as spheres of delicate operation, in which humour and humanity play a vital role in bringing perspective and levity to some of our darker moments. It is no surprise to find, in any profession, including the clerical one, that the combination of gentle, subversive scepticism mixed with compassion and pastoral wisdom *really works*. That blend allows new perspectives to emerge. You need someone to be completely serious about the fact that not all of this can be taken *too* seriously. Colonel Potter might be in charge: but we understand MASH through Hawkeye. As 2 Timothy 4.11 says: 'have Mark with you – he may be useful for your ministry'. Much as Hawkeye is essential to MASH, it is hard to imagine a Cuddesdon without Mark.

But this would not be a Cuddesdon homily without making a few closing remarks about our Gospel. For here Jesus creates a new human category for us to mull over: 'Frenemies'. We know them well in the Church, and in seminaries – people whom we are supposed to love, but loathe; folk we are meant to like, but dislike. But Jesus is uncompromising. It is no good loving those who love you. Anyone can do that. No, we have to go further to be Christian – to be Christ-like. We have to love those who do not love us.

All things considered, this is Jesus at his most radical, demanding and truthful. Until there is love for enemies, there is no real transformation of this world and in life; because the enemy always carries the dark side of our own soul. The people we sometimes dislike are usually very much like us. So Jesus instructs: we have to love our enemy to grow and mature. Sometimes that takes great humility and great compassion, but if we learn it internally, we will be prepared for what lies outside us.

So, the gospel poses a riddle. If you only love those who love you, what is the value of that? The hint from Jesus, clearly, is 'not much', the Kingdom of God cannot be built from this. War, alienation and subjugation will continue if we merely stay inside our religious or ethnic groups. We are called to leave the magnified forms of self-love and apparent safety that stop us looking to others, and yes, even at our enemies. The key to dwelling in Christ's Kingdom is to love the stranger at the gate, to love those outside our comfort zones, the outsiders, the others. Jesus says that until we can welcome the outsider, we have not truly loved at all.

What is Jesus' motivation for saying this? The wideness of God's mercy, no less. Jesus invites us to imitate God. If this is who God is and that is the way God loves, then that is how he wants us to be. The final imperative of today's Gospel is best translated by the New Jerusalem Bible. The common translation, 'be perfect' (*teleios*) is a later Greek concept that Jesus would probably not normally have used. He spoke in concrete, descriptive Aramaic metaphors, and not like a philosopher. Jesus is, however, acknowledging that his most demanding commandment is going to ask a great deal of us all: nothing less than boundless love and magnanimous grace. I cannot think of a better place to begin our study day on the future of the Church in society, and in Mark's company. For we engage here not only with critical minds, but also with soft, open hearts; and in faith, hope and charity. As the Gospel of John reminds us, 'For God so loved the world . . .'.

Article Forty-One: On Parting

The transfigured life
(Funeral address for the Revd Prof. Christopher Evans,
August 2012)

Reading: 1 Corinthians 13.

It is no surprise that, when coming to plan his funeral, Christopher asked for a very brief homily (at most), and certainly no fuss. It is typically self-effacing of the man. But when, on hearing of the passing of Christopher, Desmond Tutu interrupts his break in Honolulu to say that 'Christopher had a rich and enriching life for which we give great thanks to God – so may he rest in peace and rise in glory', you realize that keeping today low-key was always going to be a bit of a challenge. The world of New Testament scholarship could be gathered here today to pay their respects. Christopher would add, I think, with a twinkle in those Simeon-like eyes of his, that this might be a gathering of both the living and the dead of New Testament academia. His sense of humour was truly wonderful.

When debating what readings to have today, Christopher had weighed 1 Corinthians 13 with some well-known passages in Revelation. But, he had concluded, Revelation was a strange book, and oddly impenetrable even for a New Testament scholar. He once opined that it might be best read with a strobe light for company, having feasted on magic mushrooms. One of Christopher's great gifts was perspective. And even in his most prescient scholarship, he could find space for angular humour that shone light on the mind and the heart of the reader. How else can one explain his beautifully poised and tender essay in his 1971 book, *Is Holy Scripture Christian?*, in which he asks, in one essay, a question that predates our more recent absorption with all things health and safety: 'Should the New Testament be taught to children?' Christopher maintained that it was a 'thoroughly adult book'.

And so the world of the academy mourns a scholar; the Church has lost a profound mentor and formational guide; the family will miss a much-loved father, grandfather and great-grandfather. We will all miss his friendship, deeply. And despite Christopher's plea for there to be no fuss, we cannot let this day pass without commending him to God as someone who had a profound impact upon us all. One colleague recalls how Christopher taught for a few terms at Glasgow University, from 1985 to 1987. There, even in his late seventies, he taught every class with the same enthusiasm as though it was the first class he was teaching. In 18 lectures on John, it took until the eighth lecture to get out of the Prologue. Some of his witticisms are well remembered. On Pilate's saying 'What is truth?', Christopher quipped: 'Why do the pagans get all the best lines!' Christopher was a real inspiration; because of his academic, rigour coupled with a deep sense that the texts he taught had implications for the faith, life and worship of our communities.

In his own reminiscing, and in his last public lecture – entitled 'Humanity, Holiness and Humour', given at Durham in 1995 – Christopher describes his first encounter with Cuddesdon. It was not promising:

> When I was an undergraduate at Corpus Christi College, Cambridge, one of my friends proposed that we consult our theological teacher, Edwyn Hoskyns, on the subject of theological colleges. He agreed to see us, and after my friend had been in first, I followed. 'In your case, Evans,' Hoskyns said 'I think you would be well advised to consider going to Lincoln. They teach some theology there, and there is a young man named Michael Ramsey who has recently joined the staff; I think you might learn a good deal from him.' 'Now your friend', he continued, 'I have advised to go to Cuddesdon. After all Cuddesdon is for gentlemen.'

Christopher's career was remarkable. After the war he served as Chaplain of Corpus Christi College, Oxford, where he joined tutorial forces with successive counterparts at Queen's, Dennis Nineham then David Jenkins. His tutorial style formed a generation of undergraduates, including John Bowden, who later published many of his writings with SCM Press. In 1958 he was appointed Lightfoot Professor of New Testament and Canon at Durham, where he fully expected to stay until retirement, but he took up the post of Professor of New Testament at King's College, London, in 1962. His students included Desmond Tutu and a host of other church leaders. On retirement he had intended to move to rural Shropshire, but because of Elna's last illness (she passed away in 1980), they settled in Cuddesdon at Leslie Houlden's invitation, where he remained until 2008.

This passing cannot, of course, go without remarking on his Cuddesdon years. We knew here, as many had before, that Christopher had a great love for the richness of human life and an energy for relationships and things outside theology and the Church. He loved conversation, food, wine and music. Although he was very proud of his FBA and his many academic achievements, he often used to say that he would have much preferred to have been a rugby or cricket player. When he disposed of his books, all the theology went except that written by his friends. But *Wisden* remained in pride of place. All who knew him will be ever grateful for his infectious smile, his great generosity and his profound humility. Christopher fretted a great deal about whether he was a burden. But he never was, and only was, is and shall be a blessing to us here. He ended his lecture in Durham in 1995 with these words:

How do we describe what Cuddesdon meant to us? It was here that we came to know and to love, each in his own time, those who taught and guided and inspired us. It was here that the ideal of what it means to be a priest came vividly home to us. It was here that we faced the truth about ourselves before the cross of Christ, and with the painful shattering of our pride discovered that we have no sufficiency of ourselves to think anything of ourselves. And with memories solemn and searching, there mingle memories light and ludicrous, since, for all the seriousness of the purpose which brought us here we were here as human beings with our absurdities and our sense of the absurd. Learning to laugh at ourselves, we did not lack other things to laugh about. How should we, if the Christian life is indeed the knowledge of him who is the author of laughter as well as tears.

It is particularly apposite that we come to bury Christopher on the Feast of the Transfiguration. Christopher would undoubtedly concur with the Russian theologian Bulgakov (quoted in Colin Gunton's work), who says that

Things are transfigured and made luminous by beauty; they become the revelation of their own abstract meaning. And this revelation through beauty of the things of the earth is . . . art. The world, as it has been given to us, has remained as it were covered by an outward shell, through which art penetrates, as if foreseeing the coming transfiguration of the world. (Gunton, 2004, p. 142)

It is not that wisdom, beauty or God are deliberately disguised, or somehow wilfully concealed. Rather it is that we do not see properly. We miss the reality of God in its fullness. Bulgakov continues:

Transfiguration changes that. For a moment, at least, the status of everything is raised to its proper level; faces that do shine with the glory of God are seen for what they are; reflections or images of God. (Gunton, 2004, p. 142)

And so I think of Christopher's face especially today, with its warmth and radiance, and that smile. Our reading from scripture is a reminder that we are not separated from those we love by death. The Christian life has no real and ultimate 'goodbyes'; it only has 'fare-wells'. For we shall see each other again, and meet face to face. What was sown was perishable; what is raised is imperishable.

It was a pleasure and a joy that Christopher shared so much of his life with us at Cuddesdon. We loved his company. His mind remained pin-sharp to the end. In a dinner at the College to honour his centenary, he spoke without notes for over 20 minutes – powerfully and lucidly – commending the present generation of ordinands for still offering their lives to God when it was clearly so counter-cultural. And also congratulating them on their fecundity – so many children popping out left, right and centre – which clearly delighted him. And leaving us with a clarion call to ordain gay men and women, and bring the Church more fully into the twenty-first century. So we also, quite properly, celebrated the republication of Christopher's commentary on Luke's Gospel, to mark his hundredth birthday. And just as Simeon exits from Luke's Gospel, and at a great age, one suspects, so this is now our moment to say, 'Lord, now let thy servant depart in peace.'

Christopher, may you rest in peace and rise in glory.

'A word or two': humility embodied
(Funeral address for the Revd Gerald Hegarty, July 2011)

Readings: Psalm 118.13–24 and 1 Peter 5.6–11.

When God weighs a person's life, the scales don't tend to tip in favour of our achievements. Instead, God looks beneath what we have done, and asks what kind of person we have been. How have we lived our lives? How have we embodied kindness, goodness, faithfulness, self-control, humility, gentleness and patience? How have we shown warmth, compassion, justice and understanding to those who have needed our help, support and comfort?

It is not a surprise that when coming to arrange his own funeral, Gerald did not ask for a eulogy. Instead, he simply asked if I might say a word or two. When pressed as to what 'word or two' might mean, I was, to coin a phrase, 'eye-browed' by Gerald. You know what I mean: that strange way in which his eyebrow went up to somewhere between 45 and 90 degrees above his left eye, and the slight twinkle in those soft yet piercingly perceptive Irish eyes did the rest of the talking.

Whether you knew Gerald as a colleague or teacher, chaplain or vicar, husband or father, son or friend, I think essentially, we all knew the same man. He was consistent through and through. Kind, mild, gentle, wise, self-controlled, reticent, incisive; softly spoken, yet authoritative; smiling eyes and a kindly voice. Fair, moderate, temperate; modest, open-minded and generous of spirit. Yet also deeply passionate for those people, causes and issues that were so dear to him. He was a pastor's pastor. A true friend. A decent man. The best of men.

But Gerald would not have been especially interested in himself being talked about today. The invitation to say 'a word or two' was Gerald's soft and understated way of inviting us to explore the readings and music he chose, and the gospel they contain. He would want nothing less than that.

It is typically self-effacing. Don't say much about me; keep it simple; nothing too fussy. But you might want to say a word or two about the hope we have. Of course. Gerald would not have wanted his achievements listed. He, too, was more interested in the condition of the heart and the soul. He knew that true wisdom is simply to know your place before God, and your place alongside people.

Nonetheless, a few facts will help us to see who we are saying farewell to today. Gerald was born in 1952, and studied at Queen's University, Belfast, and Union Theological, Belfast. As well as a lifelong involvement with the Intercontinental Chaplains, Gerald worked initially for the University and Colleges Christian Fellowship (UCCF – the umbrella organization for student Christian Unions in higher education), supervising the travelling secretaries, and served as a non-stipendiary curate after ordination. He went on to serve as priest-in-charge of Sibson, and was a tutor at Wycliffe Hall, before his first spell as chaplain at St Edmund Hall from 1990 to 1996. He then became a much-loved tutor on the St Alban's and Oxford Ministry Course, and then it's vice-principal until 2005, having taken on his second stint as chaplain at St Edmund Hall in 2004.

When the Oxford Ministry Course joined Ripon College Cuddesdon in 2005, Gerald joined our staff too, serving with great distinction as vice-principal for the Course until quite recently. He played a vital role in ensuring the smooth transition of the Course into the life of the College, and was an amiable, wise and deeply valued colleague. I first met Gerald in 2004, as a staff member of the Oxford Ministry Course. Or, more accurately, I met one of his ordinands coming out of a lecture he had just given. 'I need to lie down now,' he said. 'Why?', I asked concerned, 'are you feeling unwell?' 'No,' he replied, 'but I have just had one hour with Gerald on the doctrine of the Trinity, and my head really hurts . . .'

He was a gifted teacher. A bit of a Mr Chips, I suppose. A brilliant educator, one who set out not to impress, but rather to explain, explore and inspire. Gerald's handouts in lectures were legendary. Literally. That is to say, rarely seen; imagined material that prompted rumour and caused much speculation. But it did not matter. No one who was taught by Gerald will ever forget his wisdom and insight, and his kindness. He was a gentle man, and generous and pastoral in his ways of getting alongside those he was teaching, taking them on, further and deeper into the mysteries of God.

But Gerald, as I say, would not have wanted his achievements or qualities listed like this. He was an intensely humble man, quiet and understated. His chosen reading for today begins, 'humble yourself . . .'; God will exalt you. God will meet you in the depths, so do not be afraid. Cast all your anxiety on him, because he cares for you. Do not be afraid. For Gerald, the currents of faith ran very deep. Perfect love casts out fear. And love and faith defined his life. In his love for God – but also for Karen, and all the family. Gerald was a man who was entirely shaped by his vocation and the values he lived by, and they shaped his relationships at every level. Gerald and Karen met 40 years ago at Queen's University, Belfast – in the library. She thought he was rather serious and too religious – at the time. But love conquers all things, even seriousness.

For in Karen and Gerald, we see two lives entwined by love, yet lives that faced outwards in gift: teaching so many, caring for all they taught, and also raising three children. Gerald was intensely proud of his children; and with Karen they managed to produce two teachers of religious studies in Richard and Charlotte, and in Matthew, a photographer who sees and interprets the world from new angles – much as Gerald did in his conversation. In Karen, also a teacher of religious studies, the dynastic line of Hegarty educators is established. The Hegartys are teachers and interpreters; education is a passion.

So to you – Karen, Richard, Matthew and Charlotte, and to Gerald's parents, Ellis and Paul, here today from Northern Ireland, to his sisters, Angela and Elizabeth, and to Kim, Sarah and George – I want to say on behalf of us all gathered here how much we share your loss, and your pain. We are all diminished by his going. We *do* know something of what you have lost in Gerald's death. But we stand with you today in prayer, solidarity and love, in shared grief – and with deep admiration for a man who brought so much to so many. He was our friend and colleague; a teacher and mentor to many; and a husband, father and a son to you. And he was a friend of God too, which meant that his life and character were marked by a particular quality that is all too rare these days.

For in the quiet, humble and understated man that was Gerald, there was also a deep radiance about him, born of a life that was touched by God. It meant he was serious, yet had levity; deep, yet with a wonderful sense of humour.

When I think of Gerald, I especially think of a man who taught and thought, loved and lived – charitably. 'Charity' comes from the Latin word *caritas* – 'costly esteem and affection' – there is a warmth and tenderness here. It is a word that resonates with 'cherishing' and 'benevolence'; the one who is charitable is the one who sees the other as dear and valued. There is diligence and duty here; but also a deep and compassionate love for the other. To live charitably is to both imagine and see the world benevolently and mercifully – as God might see it. Gerald did this, and lived it.

Gerald knew that charity – the giving of love – is an education in itself. That the teacher who is wise does not bid you to enter the house of his wisdom, but rather leads you to the threshold of your own mind, and then inspires you to go beyond. Gerald knew that the purpose of education is to replace an empty mind with an open one. And he played the long game with his students and tutees. In teaching you rarely see the fruit of a day's work. It is invisible and remains so; maybe for years, even decades. Many here today will bear testimony to that. But such a vision, and such virtues and values, are rooted in charity.

Gerald's life embodied charity. But it was also one of faith and hope. He received such care in his last days from so many at the Churchill, and the Royal Marsden – doctors, nurses and chaplains. He knew much about how he was cherished and valued by family, friends and all who cared for him. But all those who cared for him, I think, knew just how much kindness he returned.

Gerald did not want a eulogy today. He wanted a 'word or two' said, because, I think, he wanted us to know that death is not the end. In Christ, we cannot be separated from the ones we love. There is no height or depth that Christ cannot and has not overcome, so death is also conquered. Heaven is that place of clearer light and vision, where there shall be no more pain or tears. In the meantime, we bid farewell to Gerald, and mourn with Karen and all the family – for we are losing a great man. Yet Gerald would, I am sure, pray us to fare well too – in our walk with God; and in faith, hope and charity – until we meet again.

As Gerald has bid us, echoing the Psalmist, and the actual words of 1 Peter 5: 'after you have suffered a little while, the God of all grace, who has called you to his eternal glory in Christ, will himself restore, support, strengthen and establish you.' For God is love. And love is eternal. And our love for him, and his love for us, has not died with him. For in Christ, it cannot. Gerald, may you rest in peace and rise in glory. Amen.

Article Forty-Two: On Being Together

Gathering as the Church

Articles of faith, such as the Thirty-Nine Articles, came into being in order to try and bring about a peaceable state of polity in the Church. But policing a polity in any church – and one formed through a tense synthesis of theological outlooks – requires more than just articles: it needs the proponents of those views to gather, to meet and to try and resolve their differences. This in itself is not easy; indeed, it leads to more tension. It can take time. By which I don't mean months, either. This can take years, even decades; maybe more.

The worldwide Anglican Communion today contains a great many varieties of tensions. On the surface, some of the most manifest difficulties appear to be centred on issues such as sexuality, gender, the right use of the Bible, and the appropriate interpretation of scripture. But on its own, as a thesis, this is clearly inadequate, as tensions have existed within Anglicanism from the outset. There has not been a single century in which Anglicanism has not wrestled with its identity; it is by nature a polity that draws on a variety of competing theological traditions. Its very appeal lies in its own distinctive hybridity. Indeed, hybridity is an important key in understanding the wisdom of God – in Christ, his incarnate son – who chooses to work through miscibility rather than purity.

Anglicans are born of compromise; it is where we found and find God. As we noted in the Introduction, and following Luis Bermejo SJ (1989), there are four stages of ecclesial life: communication, conflict, consensus and communion. Issues in the Anglican Communion tend to get refracted through this fourfold process, as much as they do through scripture, tradition, reason and culture. This is how the Holy Spirit moves the Church; it is not the case that only the last of these stages – communion – is the 'spiritual' stage. The Holy Spirit is also manifest in conflict.

To have conflict, you have to have meetings: this is where difficulty, disagreement and acrimony are primarily encountered. But lest this sound negative, we do well to remember that Christian history, generally, is a history of progression through tense meetings. The great councils of Nicea and Chalcedon, or the debates at Worms, the Reformations in Europe, right the way through to the First and Second Vatican Councils, and to Lambeth Conferences, are gatherings of differences and diversity. These are places where ideas clash, are discerned and distilled, before slowly forming into a rich harmony infused with tension and agreement. As any parish priest knows, it is no different in the local church. Christians work through differences to find common ground. *Lex Orandi, Lex Credendi, Lex Vivendi*: As we Worship, So we Believe, So we Live.

Tense meetings then, are rather uncomfortable vehicles to sit in; but those on the journey generally reach unity. But unity is not to be confused with uniformity. The first Lambeth Conference gathered because of disunity, not unity. In 1867, as now, a number of bishops refused to come. But it was not a disaster. Conflict is not a bad thing in itself; it can be creative and point to maturity in polity that is the envy of narrower ecclesiological frames of reference. Conflict can challenge commitment and breathe life into the connections that configure communion. Church is, after all, a long-term community composed out of committed relationships. It is not a short-term project or relationship that depends on agreement in the present, let alone an immediacy of rapport. In communion – just like a good marriage – Anglicans work *through* conflict and difficulty; our faithfulness to God and one another sees to it that we find enrichment rather than weakness in our apparent tiffs and tantrums.

In focusing on the very idea of meetings – even difficult ones – we might be able to see more clearly something of the revolutionary character of the Church. This lies in the radical nature of gathering, which in turn was rooted in the revolutionary character of a theology that believed in a God who called us together to form a new community. The ecclesiology flows from the theology. Exactly how is this? To make the point more sharply, we need to understand that there are essentially two kinds of god (see Stark, 2011, pp. 9–31). The older and more primal gods are those that emerge out of communities, tribes and nations, and consecrate their habits and forms of association as virtuous and sacred. The gods of the pagan world are of this kind, and they tend to reside in shrines and other specific places, and, unless visited or called upon, do little to alter the day-to-day world of their followers. These gods look like humans, live and love like humans; and they can even be as fickle as humans.

The other kind of God does not live in a shrine. The second kind calls new communities into being. Every area of life is touched. God is infinite and beyond human thinking and emotions – indeed, beyond comprehension. The second kind of God is timeless and placeless, and there can be no image for such a deity, save perhaps the one that the Gospel of John gives us: the Word made flesh. This kind of God is indescribable. All the words and images that convey the mystery and overwhelming reality are inherently insufficient.

And there are two kinds of religions (see Stark, 2011, pp. 9–31). The first is older, and shrine-based. In ancient Rome, followers of the gods were much more like a clientele than a membership of worshippers. Clients came to temples with specific issues. But they patronized the temples and shrines; they did not belong to them. Thus, an average Roman in AD 30 might pay a visit to the temple of Zeus in the morning for one serious matter; and perhaps hoping for luck in love later on, might patronize the shrine of Aphrodite or Eros on their way home from work. The temples and shrines charged their clientele for prayers, feasts, services and rituals. And many of the temples and shrines received financial support from the State as well. The gods who dwelt therein were appealing precisely because they were quite human in their virtues, faults, passions and proclivities. And they supported the State – and the status quo.

The second kind of religion was more difficult to fathom. The religion of the monotheists made no sense to the modern world of the first-century Romans. A God who seemed distant and dif-ficult to comprehend was one problem. But the larger problem for the first-century Romans was that monotheistic faiths tended to gather crowds, or congregations. The worshippers belonged to their God, and then to one another in worship and bonded fidel-ity. Moreover, to follow this one God necessarily meant that there was one kingdom – yet to be realized – that was greater than the State. To belong to a faith that had one omnipotent ruler or God was to align oneself with a spiritual and political outlook that potentially placed the congregation above and certainly at odds with the State. The catholic ideal was, therefore, first and foremost, a vision of faith that preceded the State, and would finally triumph over temporal authority. The earthly kingdoms of the present were mere interludes.

Partly for this reason, the Romans persecuted the Zoroastrians and the Magi, who intentionally gathered together for worship. They suppressed the Bacchanalians too, who also gathered as one. Isis inspired congregations too – and the Romans suppressed them as well. Just as the Romans also suppressed the Jews, and then the Christians – who also both formed congregations. There were good reasons for the Romans to be fearful of congregations. Every meeting was, potentially, a subversive political gathering; and coming together for worship could not fail to make a socio-political statement. To some extent, you can see the traces of this problem in modern China. The State is largely happy to support Daoism, Confucian and Buddhist temples – and attendance at these shrine-based places of worship is largely done individual-istically, not corporately. So churches, which do gather people together, may need a more watchful eye from the State.

There were other reasons to fear the new congregations rooted in monotheism. The old faiths dealt with the baser senses, and were rooted in civic ceremonies, private petitions and public feasts. The new faiths – of monotheism – touched the senses in quite different ways, and were rooted in liberation, joy and even ecstasy. There was talk of love for one another, and of a God who loved creation and humanity too. No Roman seriously believed that Jupiter loved them; their gods were fickle, and to be feared. But monotheists did think that God loved them – and although God was to be feared too, God was also a redeemer.

The new monotheistic faiths also stressed individualism and vir-tue. The gods of the State were to be set aside in favour of per-sonal salvation. The monotheists believed that individuals could be saved; practices such as purification, prayer, baptism and so on emphasized this. The new faiths also had scriptures – something the old faiths lacked. The emerging new faiths were, quite suddenly, written and therefore rational. They also became organized – not only with priests, deacons and overseers, but also as distinct bodies with memberships. Congregations came into existence. Romans were infrequent and irregular visitors to their temples and shrines. The new faiths gathered intentionally, purposefully and regularly: 'when you gather . . . do this, in remembrance of me'. And this is partly what made them such a threat to the Romans. This is indeed partly why the Church, like the synagogues, were persecuted; the simple act of gathering was of itself revolutionary.

But just how radical were these gatherings? If you could travel back in time to Paul's Ephesus, you would notice, like any Mediterranean city of the day, that it was buzzing with cultural and ethnic diversity – much like our cities today. But there were some crucial differences. It was difficult to keep order in such cities. Magistrates and other officers handed out justice, but a person who was not a citizen of that city could ask to be tried by their own people under their own laws. Paul, as a Roman citizen, was able to invoke the privilege. Cities, to be well ordered, were governed by assemblies. These were sometimes called *ekklesia* – an ancient commonplace secular word from which we derive the term 'church'. And to help keep order in cities, ethnic groups who were non-citizens often lived in neighbourhoods or ghettoes. Indeed, even in modern times, we find areas of a city – sometimes called 'quarters', such as a Latin Quarter, literally meaning places to stay – for the Spaniards, French, Chinese; and sometimes for groups that are marginalized (e.g. Jewish ghetto). In ancient times, the areas reserved in a city for non-citizens were known as *paroikia* – from which we get the English word 'parish'. This is where the resident aliens lived, those who lived in the city, contributed to its welfare, but had no voting rights as such.

In the churches that Paul knew, the *ekklesia* was complex. People gathered – they assembled; in itself, unusual for a religion. In the first churches, we find Jews, Greeks and Romans, slave and free, male and female. All one in Christ. The slaves are marked with tattoos; the children run free; the men and women mix; origin and ethnicity no longer matter, for all are one in Jesus Christ. In this radical new 'assembly' of non-citizens, all are equal. Class, race, gender and age are all transcended. The 'parish church', then, is the inside place for the outsider, or as William Temple once put it, the only club that exists for non-members. This is what it means to be one in Christ: built together to be the dwelling place of God, the *oikos* – 'God's household'. The body of Christ, indeed.

Churches rarely think about the origins of their identity in this radical way. They mostly go about their business assuming their values, and implicitly imbibing these from one generation to the next. In a way, this is a pity, as valuable practices are often left to chance: inchoate by nature, they simply persist implicitly. Churches rarely think, for example, about how and why they welcome the strangers and aliens in their midst – mostly very easily, and without fuss or further reflection. But welcome they do: not only giving to the stranger, but also receiving from them. This is not merely an observation about how Christians engage with others who are not kith and kin; it is also a remark about the oft-hidden dynamic of reception, gift and charity. So just how revolutionary is the Church? Thomas Tweed observes that religions 'are confluences of organic-cultural flows that intensify joy and confront suffering by drawing on human and supra-human (i.e., divine) forces to make homes and cross boundaries' (Tweed, 2006, p. 12). I am rather drawn to this definition of religion, and by extension, of churches. Churches, at their best – and one presumes a passionate real faith in a real God as the basis for belief and practice – know that when Christians come together and gather intentionally, congregations perform four transformative roles.

First, churches intensify joy. They take the ordinary and make it extraordinary. Churches know how to celebrate lives, love and transitions. Churches bless what is good, and raise hope, thanks and expectation in prayer and praise. Congregations lift an institution and individuals to a new plane of existence – one of blessing and thankfulness for what is and can be. And worship not only moves us; it also intensifies our very being. Just as a birth becomes even more in a baptism, so in mission and ministry does a ceremony become more with prayer and celebration. Second, suffering is confronted. Working with pain, bereavement, counselling and consolation will be familiar to all ministers and churches – providing the safe space and expertise that holds and slowly resolves the suffering that individuals and institutions carry inside them. Third, the making of homes is a profoundly analogical and literal reference to the function of faith. Making safe spaces of nourishment, well-being, maturity, diversity and individuation; our 'faith homes' are places both of open hospitality and security. Fourth, faith helps us to cross boundaries – to move forward and over the challenges of life to new places. It can be crossing deserts to find promised lands, or passing from darkness to light. Religion never keeps us in one place; even with our homes, it moves us. It is in gathering that we meet the One who is present in bread and wine as we sit at table; who is there in the breaking of the bread; who makes our hearts burn as the scriptures are read. Meeting together is where we encounter Jesus Christ more richly than we can on our own. We discover the life-saving truths for the world in the radical act of our gatherings.

The Gospel of John seems to suggest that one of the key words or ideas to help us understand the ministry of Jesus and the subsequent blueprint for the Church is that of 'abiding' (see Quash, 2013). The word is linked to another English word, 'abode'. God abides with us. Christ bids us to abide in him, and he will abide in us. He bids us to make our home with him, as he has made his home with us. Christ tells us that there are many rooms in his Father's house. There are many places of gathering and meeting there. And central to the notion of an abode is the concept of abiding. To abide is to 'wait patiently with'. God has abided with us. He came to us in ordinary life, and he has sat with us, eaten with us, walked with us and lived among us. That is why John ends his Gospel with Jesus doing ordinary things: breaking bread with strangers, or eating breakfast on the seashore. God continues to dwell with us. He was with us in the beginning; and he is with us at the end. He will not leave us. And he wants his Church to abide with the world – and especially to be with all those who have no one to be with them. The friendless, the forlorn, the forgotten – God wills us to abide with them, and with each other. Fellowship is God's will for creation, not just congregations.

And that is why God is Emmanuel – God is with us. He made us for company with each other, and for eternal company with him. God is with us in creation, in redemption, and, finally, in heaven. God with us is how John's Prologue begins – the Word was with

God; he was with us in the beginning. God is with us in the valley of the shadow of death; he is with us in light and dark, chaos and order, pain and passion. And though we may turn aside from him, he will not turn from us. And in the resurrection, Jesus is again with us – more powerfully and intensely than ever. God is with us. That is the good news of the Kingdom that Jesus proclaims. We will never be left or forsaken. Whatever befalls us personally, or collectively, God will still be true to us, and hold us. And I guess that is the question for the possibility of the Church. As God is with us, can we be with each other? As God bears us all, can we bear each other? Can we truly bear the price of the Church, which is togetherness, of not being alone? For the possibility of the Church is locked up in forsaking isolation from one another. Because togetherness – deep, abiding inclusiveness, and that we should not be alone – is part of our created and redeemed world.

Ultimately, the shape of God's future Kingdom, and of our own Church, will always elude us. And this is certainly true for Anglicanism – both locally, on the ground, as well as internationally, as a communion. The apparent raggedness, as well as manifest openness and incompleteness of the Church, can be very frustrating. But it is also a profound gift. Because, for all of our ecclesiology and organization, and no matter how much we might claim our churches or denominations to be completed and perfected, born of God's nature or derived from human nurture, we need to heed Paul's injunction: 'I decided to know nothing among you except Jesus Christ and him crucified' (1 Corinthians 2.2). This is more than a declaration of some historical fact. Paul understands the crucifixion of Christ in cosmic terms: it stretches from the present to the very end of time. And so the Christ whom we know in the Church – the only one we can know – is the One who was crucified and raised. But even when raised, still bears the marks of crucifixion. And he is with us.

The first disciples were deeply troubled by this. They expected to see Christ manifest in some form of triumphant glory. But it was not so. The Christ who is revealed on the cross is the same who is revealed in the resurrection. The fullness of the revelation lies in the continuity. And this means that the Church bears scars, wounds, pain and suffering in its ongoing life. The Church – as wounded, but raised – is the body of Christ. The glory of God, it seems, will be made manifest in our weak and powerless states, not just our strengths and gifts. We find God in differences and in conflict, as well as in consensus and communion. The glory of Anglicanism lies, ironically, partly in its dependency and its incompleteness, as well as in its reformed catholicity. It lies in its breadth and depth; a pale reflection, no less, of God's omnipresence and all-encompassing love. To paraphrase one writer:

Why do I, who once upon a time found the Anglican Church so boring that I detached myself as a young teenager (and so went off in search of certitude and excitement in religion), now find it so enchanting? Why do I now find the Anglican Church, in all its breadth, hybridity and miscibility, such a source of hope? Why do I love it? Let me count the ways . . .

I love it because it is patient. It does not expect the world to change in an instant, or to be bludgeoned into belief, because it knows that certain things take centuries.

I love it because it is kind. It is kind enough to welcome strangers, whatever their beliefs, and shake their hands, and offer them a coffee after church.

I like the fact that it is neither envious (of more flamboyant, more attention-seeking and more successful-at-proselytising religions), nor boastful.

I like the fact that it is not arrogant or rude. I like the fact that it does not insist on its own way, but is genuinely tolerant of other religious beliefs – and none.

I like the fact that it does not rejoice in wrongdoing, but quietly presents an ethical framework of kindness.

I like the fact that it believes in the values of the New Testament, and of St Paul's description of love, which I've just paraphrased, but also believes that it is more important to embody them than to quote them.

I like the fact that it doesn't speak like a child, think like a child, or reason like a child. I like the fact that it is mature enough to value faithful doubt.

I like the fact that it is calm. I like the fact that it recognises that the religious impulse is here to stay, and that the more you try to crush it, the stronger it will become. And that all human beings, irrespective of their beliefs, have yearnings for the transcendent.

And I like the fact that although secured in scripture, tradition and reason, it is not afraid to seek and find God in our wider culture – in art, literature, nature and in society.

(C. Patterson, 2009, p. 24)

This may all seem like an argument – as a genre of posters, coasters and other cultural ephemera currently proclaims – to 'Keep Calm and Carry On'. And to some extent that is indeed my counsel for Anglican polity. The Church will survive. It is God's body. He will not neglect his own body. And that is precisely why gathering matters so much for churches and denominations, even when we are not quite sure of our moorings any more, and perhaps even fear that we no longer belong together.

Just ask the disciples who, when all seemed lost, didn't split up and go their separate ways. They still gathered together in an upper room and waited for what must have seemed like an eternity. But wait together they did, for the promise of the Spirit to come upon them. And two other unknown disciples, walking together one late afternoon, still in grief and shock at the loss of their Messiah, and after a long hike up the road to Emmaus, invited a stranger who had strolled with them to share in their simple supper. Anglicans know how that story ends. In breaking bread together, the Lord is here.

Dates and Sources for Articles

1   'Reloading the Trinity', *Guardian*, Saturday 14 June 2003.
2   'A Gift at the Turning of the Year', *Guardian*, Saturday 1 January 2005.
3   'Unholy Words for Holy Week', *Independent*, Saturday 7 April 2002.
4   'Easter Facts and Fictions', *Guardian*, Saturday 10 April 2004 and 'New Beginnings in an Empty Tomb', *Guardian*, Saturday 19 April 2003.
5   'Pentecost and Speaking in Tongues', a sermon preached at Christ Church Cathedral, Oxford, 2007.
6   Turl Street Arts Festival Sermon, Jesus College, Oxford, Hilary Term 2007.
7   From two homilies for BBC Radio Four, broadcast for Vocations Sunday, 29 April 2012.
8   'Anglican Life, Catholic Identity', *Guardian*, Saturday 10 February 2007.
9   'All Desires Known', *Guardian*, Saturday 1 December 2007.
10 'Father of the Man', *Guardian*, Saturday 17 June 2002.
11 'The Mother of All Days', *Guardian*, Saturday 9 March 2002.
12 'The Stranger at the Gate', *Guardian*, Saturday 10 November 2001.
13 Sermon for the Commencement of Term for the Oxford Ministry Course, September 2010.
14 Sermon for those leaving College, June 2010.
15 Sermon for those joining College, September 2010.
16 Sermon for those beginning ordination training, September 2009.
17 'Who Do you Say That I Am?' A sermon for the start of the new academic year, September 2009.

18 Sermon on healing mission, September 2006.

19 'Why Dr Sentamu Cut Up His Dog-Collar', *Guardian*, 11 December 2007.

20 From the *Guardian*, Saturday 12 November 2005 and a sermon for Remembrance Sunday 2012.

21 A homily for the blessing and dedication of the new Edward King Chapel at Ripon College, Cuddesdon, February 2013, on the Eve of Candlemas.

22 'A Harvest of the Spirit', *Guardian*, Saturday 11 September 2004.

23 'God's Cry for England and St George', *Guardian*, Saturday 23 April 2005.

24 'Arguments for the Church', *Guardian*, Saturday 4 November 2006.

25 'Praying for Unity?', *Guardian*, Saturday 21 January 2006.

26 'Breaking Up is Hard to Do', *Guardian*, Saturday 11 October 2003.

27 'Call Off the Canon Fire', *Guardian*, Saturday 12 July 2003.

28 Homily for the Week of Prayer for Christian Unity, 2007.

29 'The House Built on Flexi-Rock – Hope for the Anglican Communion', a sermon for Great St Mary's, Cambridge, May 2005.

30 Adapted from the *Daily Telegraph*, 21 November 2012.

31 Sermon preached at Ripon College, Cuddesdon, 3 November 2009.

32 Sermon preached at Ripon College, Cuddesdon, June 2010.

33 Sermon for leavers on the Patron Saint of Encouragement, June 2011.

34 Sermon Preached at Ripon College, Cuddesdon, 21 September 2008.

35 A commemoration for a mystic at the end of term.

36 Leavers' sermon, 8 June 2012.

37 Sermon for leavers, June 2011.

38 Drawn from a sermon at Lincoln Cathedral, March 2010, commemorating the centenary of Edward King's death; and more recently at the first Eucharist celebrated in the

new Edward King Chapel at Ripon College, Cuddesdon, on King's commemoration day, 8 March 2013.

39 Sermon preached for Oxford Theological Colleges, March 2011.

40 Homily on Richard Hooker (the other one) and Mark (again, the other one): commemorating 20 years of the Revd Prof. Mark Chapman's ministry at Cuddesdon, November 2011.

41 Funeral oration for the Revd Prof. Christopher Evans, New Testament scholar and priest, who died in July 2012, aged 101. Funeral at All Saints' Parish Church, Cuddesdon, 6 August 2012, Feast of the Transfiguration. The funeral address for the Revd Gerald Hegarty, Tutor in Doctrine and former Vice-Principal of the Oxford Ministry Course, given at St Andrew's Church, Oxford, 1 July 2011.

42 From a lecture given to seminarians at St John's College, Auckland, New Zealand, April 2013.

The Thirty-Nine Articles (1662)

1   Of Faith in the Holy Trinity.
2   Of Christ the Son of God.
3   Of his going down into Hell.
4   Of his Resurrection.
5   Of the Holy Ghost.
6   Of the Sufficiency of the Scripture.
7   Of the Old Testament.
8   Of the Three Creeds.
9   Of Original or Birth-sin.
10   Of Free-Will.
11   Of Justification.
12   Of Good Works.
13   Of Works before Justification.
14   Of Works of Supererogation.
15   Of Christ alone without Sin.
16   Of Sin after Baptism.
17   Of Predestination and Election.
18   Of obtaining Salvation by Christ.
19   Of the Church.
20   Of the Authority of the Church.
21   Of the Authority of General Councils.
22   Of Purgatory.
23   Of Ministering in the Congregation.
24   Of speaking in the Congregation.
25   Of the Sacraments.
26   Of the Unworthiness of Ministers.
27   Of Baptism.
28   Of the Lord's Supper.
29   Of the Wicked which eat not the Body of Christ.

30 Of both kinds.

31 Of Christ's one Oblation.

32 Of the Marriage of Priests.

33 Of Excommunicate Persons.

34 Of the Traditions of the Church.

35 Of the Homilies.

36 Of Consecrating of Ministers.

37 Of Civil Magistrates.

38 Of Christian men's Goods.

39 Of a Christian man's Oath.

References and Further Reading

Adams, D. (1982), *Life, the Universe, and Everything*, London: Pan.

Andrewes, L. (1903), *The Preces Privatae of Lancelot Andrewes, Bishop of Winchester*, trans. with notes F. E. Brightman, London: Methuen.

Bermejo sj, L. (1989), *The Spirit of Life: The Holy Spirit in the Life of the Christian*, Chicago, IL: Loyola University Press.

Brown, Dan (2003), *The Da Vinci Code*, New York: Bantam Press.

Brown, David (2000), *Discipline and Imagination: Christian Tradition and Truth*, Oxford: Oxford University Press.

Browning, E. Barrett (2008), *Aurora Leigh*, Oxford: Oxford Paperbacks.

Bryson, B. (1995), *Notes from a Small Island*, New York: Doubleday.

Butterworth, N. and Inkpen, M. (2008), *Jasper's Beanstalk*, London: Hodder.

Coakley, S. (ed.) (1997), *Religion and the Body*, Cambridge: Cambridge University Press.

Camara, H. (1974), *The Desert is Fertile*, London: Sheed & Ward.

Congar, Y. (1950), *True and False Reform in the Church*, Paris: Editions du Cerf.

Cupitt, D. (1991), *What is a Story?* London: SCM Press.

Davis, K. (1990), *Emancipation Still Comin': Explorations in Caribbean Emancipatory Theology*, New York: Orbis Books.

de Botton, A. (14 March 2010), *The School of Life: On Gratitude*, www.schooloflife.com.

de Waal, E. (1984), *Seeking God: The Way of St Benedict*, London: Fount.

Evans, C. (1971), *Is Holy Scripture Christian? And Other Questions*, London: SCM Press.

Fasheh, M. (1992), 'Reclaiming Our Identity and Redefining Ourselves' in N. Atteek, M. Ellis and R. Radford Ruether (eds), *Faith and the Intifada*, New York: Orbis.

Fox, K. (2004), *Watching the English: The Hidden Rules of English Behaviour*, London: Hodder & Stoughton.

Fraser, G. (2012), 'Goodbye, St Paul's. Hello, St Mary's', *Guardian*, 4 May.

Grierson, D. (1985), *Transforming a People of God*, Melbourne: Joint Board of Christian Education of Australia and New Zealand.

Gunton, C. (2004), *The Doctrine of Creation*, London: Continuum.

Hardy, D. W. and Ford, D. F. (1984), *Jubilate: Theology in Praise*, London: Darton, Longman & Todd.

Herbert, G. (2004), *The Complete Poems of George Herbert*, London: Penguin.

Hervieu-Leger, D. (2000), *Religion as a Chain of Memory*, Cambridge: Polity Press.

Holmes, U. T. (1982), *What is Anglicanism?* Wilton, CT: Morehouse-Barlow.

Hooker, R. (1989), *Of the Laws of Ecclesiastical Polity*, Cambridge: Cambridge University Press.

John of the Cross (2008), *Ascent of Mount Carmel*, trans. and ed. E. Allison Peers, Radford, VA: Wilder Publications.

Jones, G. (2013), 'Games and Stories: Poem for Holy Saturday' (unpublished).

Lamott, A. (1995), *Bird by Bird: Some Instructions on Writing and Life*, New York: Anchor Books.

Lamott, A. (2000), *Travelling Mercies: Some Thoughts on Faith*, New York: Anchor Books.

Lederach, J.-P. (2006), *The Moral Imagination: The Art and Soul of Peacemaking*, Oxford: Oxford University Press.

Maclean, N. (1976), *A River Runs Through It and Other Stories*, Chicago, IL: University of Chicago Press.

Macmurray, J. (1970), *The Form of the Personal: Persons in Relation*, London: Faber, 1970.

McConnell, T. (1983), 'Anglican Identity', in P. Elmen (ed.), *The Anglican Moral Choice*, Wilton, CT: Morehouse.

McDowell, J. (1981), *Evidence that Demands a Verdict*, London: Scripture Union.

McLaren, B. (2004), *Generous Orthodoxy*, Grand Rapids, MI: Zondervan.

Miller, K. (2007), *There is an Anger that Moves*, London: Carcanet Press.

Packer, J. (1958), 'The Fundamentalism Controversy: Retrospect and Prospect', *Faith and Thought* 90 (1), vol. 11.

Patten, B. (1996), 'Minister for Exams', in B. Patten, *Armada*, London: HarperCollins.

Patterson, C. (2009), *Independent*, 29 July.

Patterson, W. B. (2000), 'Richard Hooker's Theology for Our Time', *Sewanee Theological Review* 43 (4), pp. 503–11.

Percy, M. (1999), *Introducing Richard Hooker and the Laws of Ecclesiastical Polity*, London: Darton, Longman & Todd.

Pickard, S. (2012), *Seeking the Church: An Introduction to Ecclesiology*, London: SCM Press.

Pritchard, J. (2006), *The Life and Work of a Priest*, London: SPCK.

Quash, B. (2013), *Abiding: The Archbishop of Canterbury's Lent Book*, London: Bloomsbury.

Radcliffe, T. (2010), 'Why go to church? The drama of the Eucharist', *The Oxford Theologian*, Spring edition, Oxford: University of Oxford.

Ramsey, M. (1972), *The Christian Priest Today* (2nd imp. edn), London: SPCK.

Rilke, R. M. (1905), *The Book of Hours: Love Poems to God*, New York: Camden House Publishing.

Selby, P. (1997), *Grace and Mortgage: The Language of Faith and the Debt of the World*, London: Darton, Longman & Todd.

Stark, R. (2011), *The Triumph of Christianity*, New York: HarperCollins.

Taylor, D. (1996), *The Healing Power of Story*, New York: Doubleday.

Thompson, F. (1998), *The Hound of Heaven and Other Poems*, New York: Branden Publishing.

Tweed, T. (2006), *Crossing and Dwelling*, Cambridge, MA: Harvard University Press.

Visser, M. (2001), *The Geometry of Love: Space, Time, Mystery, and Meaning in an Ordinary Church*, New York: North Point Press.

Wallis, J. (1994), *The Soul of Politics: A Practical and Prophetic Vision for Change*, Maryknoll, NY: Orbis Books.

Williams, R. (2002), *Writing in the Dust: A Meditation on September 11*, London: Hodder & Stoughton.